PRACTICAL *GARDEN* GUIDES

Growing Herbs Successfully

VIOLET STEVENSON

TIGER BOOKS INTERNATIONAL
LONDON

Editor: Susanne Mitchell
Designer: John Fitzmaurice
Picture research:
   Moira McIlroy

This edition published
in 1989 by Tiger Books
International PLC, London

Produced by
Marshall Cavendish Books Ltd
58 Old Compton Street
London W1V 5PA

ISBN 1 85501 001 1

Printed and bound in Portugal

CONTENTS

INTRODUCTION

INTRODUCTION

Below Redolent of medieval times this modern herb garden follows tradition with a formal geometric layout. Early herbalists made intricate patterns in the garden by separating clumps of plants with brick paving and later with low hedges. Their main concern, though, was to produce a design that was functional so that herbs could be picked with ease. *Opposite* A herb garden that is more informal but still easily accessible to cooks and gardeners

SCENTED PLANTS STIR the imagination, for there is something magical about a leaf which, when bruised between the fingers or accidentally pressed underfoot, even brushed in passing, releases a sweet, tangy, pungent or perhaps savoury scent. Most gardens contain one or more kinds of such plants which have come to be known popularly as herbs. In some gardens they are an important feature and may even have a specially designed area devoted to them.

The cultivation and use of herbs, like the rose, roams so many centuries that it is impossible to go back to its origins. However, we know from the many records that have been left by ancient peoples that the use of herbs was widespread and constant. They were used, for instance, in medicine, lotions, ointments, cosmetics, embalming, religion, love potions, magic and, of course, in cooking.

HERBS IN HISTORY

It may be difficult, living in our modern sanitised surroundings, for us to imagine the foul odours and stench which must once have prevailed in communities of people, at least at certain times of the year, but by doing so we can understand why the most sweetly scented plants were liberally gathered and used in a variety of ways to create a fresher scent near and around one.

Where wild herbs abounded, they were gathered from the countryside, but eventually roots and cuttings of some were brought home and planted.

Herbs and Food

It may also be hard for some of us to appreciate the difficulties of keeping food untainted without the benefits of refrigeration, a situation which existed until quite recent times. The wealthy might have been able to afford to build icehouses and to stock them with ice in the winter for use in summer. Those with wells could use their cool depths to hold lowered butter, milk and meat for short periods, but the majority, when they had meat or fish to keep or preserve, would need to salt or pickle it in some other way if it were not to be used freshly killed.

A long winter diet of salted and pickled foods without the modern variety of fresh green vegetables and diverse fruits would lead to a sameness in the taste of dishes, a very monotonous diet, unless some other strong flavour could be introduced. This is where herbs came to play their part. Strongly flavoured they had to be and at one time they were used

Above Illustrations from Gerard's *Herbal* published in 1597

in such quantities as would not now, with our more sensitive palates, be acceptable. For instance fennel, a strong 'up-market' herb today so far as most people are concerned, was greatly favoured and used liberally for dishes other than fish, for which it is more usually reserved now.

Many herbs were believed to have prophylactic properties. Others were considered to be good for the digestion. In both cases these would be natural choices for long-hung game or for meat which one feared had been kept too long or under too warm conditions. Yet conversely some herbs would help to flavour, and to make more tender, meat which had been freshly killed and might consequently be tough or tasteless. They were useful also in flavouring the fresh-water fish which sometimes, and especially in periods of drought, are liable to taste a little 'muddy'. These could be made much more palatable when they were stuffed with, poached or marinated in, herbs.

Herbs in Medicine

While it may seem to us now that culinary herbs were of great importance, it was, in fact, those that had a medicinal value which were at first most sought after and valued. Such plants were dried so that they might be readily available at all times of the year and so that they could be transported easily and sold freely in towns and cities or in those localities where they were not to be found growing freely. It is an interesting link with the past that the word drug, now often used in a modern context for many substances far removed from plant materials, is a part of the Anglo-Saxon word '*drigan*', to dry.

The Role of the Monasteries

Travellers abroad brought home to their native countries not only the herb plants or seeds themselves, but also knowledge of the ways in which they were used in other countries. Since most travellers were drawn from the more learned section of a people, this greater knowledge, which was constantly added to, passed mainly into the hands of those who could write and also teach and whose role in life was often to minister to

the sick and needy. Thus it is that we find in medieval times that it is the monks in most countries who were the most informed herbalists.

When we consider the communication that existed between religious houses, not only in different parts of a country but also between countries, we can be sure that many herbs exchanged hands in one form or another.

A productive garden was an essential part of monastic life, so it would be logical that it should give space to those plants which were valued for their medicinal virtues as well as their culinary worth. Many of the flowers used for decorating the church during festivals were also herbal and many were used in salads, broths and sweetmeats to add colour as well as taste.

From the monks, and most likely under their guidance, the practice of growing, using and distributing herbs passed also to the ladies of the castles who would ensure that there were sufficient plants near at hand to supply the still room, in many ways the power house of the household, which was often as busy as a kitchen. Here herbs — and these included many flowers not always grouped under the title of 'herb' today — were dried, pounded, distilled, blended, conserved and otherwise preserved in many diverse ways.

Formal Herb Gardens

One assumes that once ladies began to take an interest in gardening it was natural that they should wish the plants to fall into neat and tidy patterns and that it was in this manner that the formal herb garden began gradually to take shape. Those who did not come to this style of gardening through natural talent could find plenty of guidance, for more and more books came to be written on the subject, with the result that more and more gardens were laid out to plan. One writer suggested that the parterres should be filled with flowers and various plants and edged with dwarf hedges of sweet-scented, low-growing plants such as lavender, thyme, marjoram and many others. This is a plan which would have greatly appealed to the neat, methodical and frugal, because the edgings would need to be clipped to keep them low and in order and, of course, the clippings would not be wasted but would be used in some way.

'Magic' Herbs

Like so many other examples of natural phenomena, plants — and especially herbs — were subject to superstition. Certainly they played their part in magical rites and were also used, often by the village 'wise woman', in the concoction of love potions and aphrodisiacs. Many of the superstitions and practices in which these particular plants featured lingered on into the Victorian era, and indeed some may still exist. But in Britain the majority lost their significance during the Commonwealth, being considered anti-Puritan.

The Changing Role of Herbs

After this period it seemed that the significance of so many plants once considered of great importance began to wane. A smaller number of almost universally approved herbs such as parsley, tarragon, rosemary, chervil, thyme and sage, lingered on to join the ever expanding numbers of exotic kinds, mainly spices, which were imported from other countries as foreign trade expanded. This remains true today when a growing interest in the national dishes of immigrant people causes a familiar herb to take on a new importance. A good example is coriander, which for the British had always been considered a spice, since only its sweetly flavoured seeds were used, but further East the fresh green leaves, also sometimes known as Chinese parsley or cilantro, are widely used and the roots of the plant are introduced into certain curry pastes. This has resulted in a demand for fresh coriander.

In so limited a space it is impossible to do more than present a wide and general concept of the changing role of the importance of herbs. Certainly a change in gardening styles exercised a great influence. Other plants came to be more highly regarded than the more utilitarian herbs, although the prettiest of these continued to be favoured and often hybridised to take modern forms.

Dried herbs have enjoyed an increasing popularity over a number of years until the present day when a new interest in herbs and their uses has arisen. But dried herbs have not the same quality as fresh ones: to some people they prove to be indigestible. Fortunately, discerning cooks and those who enjoy their meals either know or are discovering that there is really nothing to replace freshly gathered herbs. Fortunately also few plants are easier to grow than most of the popular kinds.

Those who find room for a collection of herbs in the garden, no matter how modest this may be, will soon find that they have provided themselves with the means of producing the right-tasting traditional dishes but also a most useful complement for many of our mass-produced foods. Quantities of these are deep frozen, and often on thawing and cooking they do not prove as flavoursome as expected, yet by applying the right herbs it is often possible to transform the dish.

Culinary plants, though, are not the whole herb story. In a world where we are daily surrounded by strong commercially produced 'scents', an old-fashioned potpourri blended from home-grown flowers will bring unlimited pleasure. So, too, will a gift of a herb pillow to the sleepless or bed linen scented by lavender bags laid in the drawer or cupboard — to mention only a few delights. And for those who suffer from headaches, strain or minor ailments, how reassuring to know that a tisane made from a favourite garden plant is likely to be just as efficacious as a tablet from a chemist's bottle.

Below A herb garden based on a medieval plan, with informal clumps of herbs round a geometric centrepiece of box hedge

1 *Rosa* 'Dagmar Hastrup'
2 *Rosa eglanteria*
3 *Hosta sieboldiana*
4 Common marjoram
5 Mint
6 Balm
7 Horseradish
8 Burnet
9 Basil
10 Parsley
11 Chives
12 Gooseberry
13 *Rubus trilobus*
14 *Paeonia officinalis*
15 Dill
16 Strawberries
17 *Rubus phoenicolasius*
18 Sweet cicely
19 *Chamaecyparis obtusa* 'Nana Gracilis'
20 *Ilex* 'Veitchii'
21 Summer savory
22 Hyssop
23 Chervil
24 Thyme
25 Sage
26 *Lilium longiflorum*
27 Rhubarb
28 *Petasites japonicus giganteus*
29 *Lavandula spica*
30 *Buxus sempervirens*
31 *Rosa* 'Peace'
32 *Ruta graveolens*
33 Lovage
34 Sorrel
35 *Asperula odorata*
36 Fennel
37 *Vaccinium corymbosum*
38 *Juniperus squamata* 'Meyeri'

CHAPTER ONE

HERBS IN THE GARDEN

Opposite The subtle colours and varied forms of the herbs planted at the Royal Horticultural Society's headquarters in Wisley produce a border which has pleasing visual qualities as well as botanical interest

WHAT CHARACTERISTICS DISTINGUISH a 'herb' from other plants? To confuse the issue, the term has two meanings. Botanically, and incidentally most anciently, 'a herb is a plant of which the stem dies to the ground at the end of the season. Herbs may be annual, biennial or perennial.' So, correctly and in gardening terms, a herb may be any herbaceous plant. However, there are many familiar and popularly named 'herbs', such as lavender, rosemary, thyme and sage, which are shrubs, and in the case of the bay, even a tree. These do not fit the botanical description. Instead they fall into the looser, popular meaning of the term, which to the majority of people covers those plants whose leaves are used for various purposes, including food, drink, medicine, flavouring, scent and even dyes.

Spices and Seeds

Spices differ from herbs in that, although they are derived from plants, they are not leafy. They may be seeds, bark as in cinnamon, or an aril as in mace, which is the membrane wrapper around the nutmeg, or flower buds as are cloves and capers. Only a few of the plants grown as herbs in the garden also produce spices in the form of seeds, for not all herb plant seeds are wholesome. Fennel seeds are good to eat and green sweet cicely seeds can be chopped and used in salads. Angelica seeds can be used for flavouring sweets. Caraway and poppies are grown for their seeds alone. The poppy, which provides such rich, black, oily seeds used in bread and cake making, is *Papaver somniferum*, actually the opium poppy, a long-time favourite garden plant since it

is so handsome and also because it has produced many lovely double-flowered forms which look like paeonies.

SITING THE HERB GARDEN

As mentioned in the introduction, herb gardens were created in order that many of the plants which were used in a number of different ways both domestically and medicinally were near at hand when required, or in order to facilitate harvesting.

In the early days of this century, cottage gardeners almost always had a few herbs — rosemary, sage and thyme — growing near the door, usually in a little border closely jostled by some favourite flowering kinds. Here the herbs were not only conveniently near for the cook, but also near enough to the door for the cottager to be able quickly to pick a bunch to press into a parting visitor's hand 'for friendship and flavour'.

Otherwise herbs would be planted, still not far from the cottage door, but at the side of the path which led to the vegetable plot, so that having selected the vegetables for the day, the requisite herb or herbs could also be gathered on the way back to the house. Most beehives would have balm planted nearby, for there was a belief among bee keepers that this lemon-scented plant helped bees to find their way home.

In the present day, the wide range and variety of herbs makes it easy to introduce them into the design of the average garden. They are simply to be regarded and treated in the same way as any other garden plants. Although there is one important point to be borne in mind when

Below The opium poppy is famous for its medicinal properties, being a source also of heroin and morphine. Today, however, the plant is harvested from most gardens for the tiny black seeds which are used to decorate cakes and bread rolls

deciding upon their position: herbs are to be cut frequently, so they should be easily accessible, planted near the front of the border or within arm's reach.

Those who are not intent on creating a strictly formal herb garden, or perhaps a plot which is to contain only culinary herbs, will discover that it is possible to furnish a garden, even the greatest part of it, entirely with plants which are scented in some or all parts. In addition to the generally accepted herbs, these can range from annuals such as mignonette or tobacco flower, biennials such as Brompton stock, wallflowers and sweet williams, perennials like sweet bergamot and scented geranium, *G. microrrhizum*, to shrubs such as cistus with scented leaves, mock orange and old-fashioned roses, all with deliciously scented blooms.

Herbal plants need not be confined to the border, for the margins of a pond or any other moist land can hold meadow-sweet, tansy, sweet flag, angelica, peppermint and black mint and comfrey.

Below The old fashioned cottage garden plant *Reseda odorata*, or mignonette, has inconspicuous but fragrant blossoms. They appear throughout the summer and are valued as cut flowers for bouquets

Soil, Sun and Shade

Generally speaking the specialist lays down fairly strict rules on the correct situation for the different herbs, usually stating definitely which should be grown in sun and which in shade, and there are instructions to this effect in the chapter beginning on page 36. However, in case this should deter the new gardener who may not have the choice of many sites, as well as to add a personal note, it is interesting to find — where herbs are allowed to grow very much as they wish, as they do in one area in my own garden, on a long bank running from east to west — that those such as the mints, for instance, which are said to prefer some shade and which were originally planted on the north side, find their way over to the sunny side where they flourish luxuriantly, sometimes too luxuriantly, although they suffer from drought from time to time. It is also interesting to see how self-sown seedlings of thyme, balm, lavender, marjoram, appear, not in the deep, rich soil provided, but in the sandy gravel between the paving stones of the path running alongside the bank. So there is no need to be too closely bound by horticultural rules if these are difficult to meet.

However, there is no doubt that if the gardener wishes to produce the freshest, most succulent leaves of such plants as the various mints, parsley, including the parsnip-rooted Hamburg variety, chervil, sweet cicely and angelica, some shade, root moisture and rich soil will give the best results. If the shrubby herbs and sub-shrubs such as marjoram are to be at their most pungent they will need as much sunshine as they can get. Provided the soil is good — and good soil can always be imported — a shady town backyard, for instance, is more likely to produce satisfactory angelica, sweet cicely, parsley, mint and chervil, to list but few, than a sun-baked balcony or patio, on which thymes, and sages and other labiates should thrive more luxuriantly and pungently than they would in the shade.

The best thing to do, obviously, is to assess any area where it is hoped that herbs can be grown and note which are the sunniest and which the shadiest sites and to plant accordingly. This may mean dividing the herb garden into two parts or distributing the herbs about the garden rather than planting them in one place.

DISPLAYING HERBS

Fortunately there exists so much variety among herbs that the gardener should be able to find plants suitable for almost every situation. If the selection is to extend beyond the culinary kinds, then one could expect to create a very attractive and interesting garden, no matter how small the plot may be.

Herbs as Edgings

Traditionally, parsley seemed to be the only herb to be grown in a row among the other conventionally spaced vegetables; certainly it was the herb most often and most liberally used, for making country wine as well as flavouring. Quite often it was used as an edging along a path.

This remains one of the most convenient and attractive ways of growing this herb. It can be used as a summer edging around a flower bed. Prettily leaved, it mixes well with other plants, providing a pleasant contrast of textures.

Those gardeners who have little space to spare in a food plot or elsewhere might consider making a productive and interesting edging by mixing herbs, using together all those which are of roughly the same height, for instance parsley, chives and thyme. Plant them alternately along the length of the edging. For greater variety space could be left between the plants for basil or some kind which has to be raised indoors and planted out after the frosts. The fact that all of these will be cut fairly regularly means that the edging will be kept neat.

Growing Herbs in Rows

Although some herbs suit informal settings, it is more practical to grow many of them in formal rows. This applies to those, such as chervil, which are to be grown in succession, or such as caraway which is to be harvested for its seeds.

Above A variety of herbs planted in restricted space can, but need not, resemble a confusion of weeds. Treated like the occupants of any herbaceous bed, and arranged informally but within an overall design, they can provide a strong focal point, particularly in the small garden

Left Patches of herbs which include marjoram, poppies and chives, will provide a splash of colour in summer, and maybe novelty amongst the permanent features of a shrub border, or vegetable plot

11

Herb Hedges

But to be formal does not necessarily mean to be without charm. There are many ways in which formal patterns can be applied to add attraction and interest to a garden. For example, rows of one kind of shrubby herb, lavender, rosemary, santolina and sage for instance, can be used as low hedges to divide one part of a garden from another, or perhaps to lead the way to a special herb garden. Incidentally, the sides of paths are usually well drained and the soil close to their edges consequently warmer than elsewhere in the border. It is often cold winter wet at their roots which affects and kills some of the exotic herbs, expecially those from the Mediterranean regions, so it is important that the soil around their roots should be well drained and kept as warm as possible. This is one reason why a pathside planting is beneficial, apart from the fact that it is often the most convenient, making it easier to carry out such operations as clipping and harvesting.

Lavender looks particularly well grown this way and, of course, contributes greatly to the garden colour when the plants are in bloom. At this time it attracts a great many butterflies and other insects which visit the flowers for nectar. Do not be in a hurry to cut off faded flower heads, for the seeds will attract finches and other little birds in winter. Furthermore, this is a plant which will naturally seed itself freely if allowed to do so, a pleasant characteristic of many herbs, which means that the gardener always has a few plants to pass on to other would-be herbalists.

Patios and Paving

Shrubby herbs are ideal for small enclosed gardens and for patios, so long as they get the sun. Somehow their scent seems more intense when they are enclosed in this manner. A rosemary bush will grow quite large in time but where there is little space to spare in a patio, the plant can actually be trained to cover a wall, and it and others can be grown in containers.

Paved and shingled areas are ideal situations for the sun-loving herbs. Indeed, for the gardener who is looking for an easy-to-maintain yet still productive type of garden, a shingled area devoted to herbs could prove to be very rewarding. Bays or beds for those kinds which have to be annually seeded, such as parsley, could easily be made in the shadier sections.

Some herbs, thymes, pennyroyal, common marjoram for instance, are very low-growing, although their flower stems may rise above the main level of the plant. Some are prostrate, some simply sprawling and some cushion-forming. By using them and exploiting their characteristics it is possible to furnish attractively a paved or stony area, either to break up a monotonous mass or to soften harsh edges.

Sometimes it may be best to remove a paving stone or two, or alternatively, if they are small enough, plants can be introduced into a very small space between stones. Their roots will soon go down between the stones and spread out widely beneath them, and at the same time the leafy upper part will travel out from its original spot until it covers quite a large area. Some will cascade down over the edge of a raised bed and lavender and rosemary, perhaps surprisingly, are two that will grow prettily this way. Both of these can be grown in the space made by removing a paving stone. Marjoram will make a good, leafy carpet on stone or over it. In my own garden it seeds itself in the cracks between the paving.

Creeping and carpeting thymes are both useful and pretty for this purpose. I use them in combination with rectangular paving stones set about 30cm (1ft) apart as a path running alongside the herb bank. The thymes have been planted in the spaces between each stone, their roots directed down into the soil below the gravel and sand spread on

Below Well defined areas for herbs can be created by edging the beds with brick, pebbles or even sunken railway sleepers. Allowing plants to overspill onto paths softens the harsh appearance of shingle 'covers' laid to provide easy access and some warmth to the beds

the surface between the paving slabs. The spreading stems root into this as they grow. The plants have gradually spread to fill the spaces, giving an attractive, soft, chequered appearance to the strip, mainly green and grey-green according to the variety or species of thyme, and at times smothered with purple, pink or white flowers.

Paths and Lawns

Where there is not to be a great deal of traffic, an entire path around a herb garden can be covered with creeping herbs. Pennyroyal, one of the mint species, can be used this way, particularly in a sheltered garden where there is also a little shade and moist soil, for an exposed, sunny place and frosts are not so good for this species.

The carpeting thymes are sometimes used to create little lawns, for instance in the centre of a circular herb garden.

Chamomile also, either alone or with grass, is used for lawns and is said to make a really good, tough sward which will withstand considerable traffic, as do some of the lawns at Buckingham Palace where these plants are used together. This is a good choice for seaside gardens, especially those fairly close to the water.

Ground Cover

Many herbs of the larger kinds, apart from those that are prostrate, will cover ground often quite tenaciously and for this reason they can be used for banks where they will not only cover the soil but also hold it firm and prevent it from sliding down. Obviously those with creeping roots are best for this purpose, mints and tansy for instance. In a large garden a good choice is the native soapwort. This produces generous clusters of softly scented pink flowers that show a marked resemblance to the double pinks which are members of the same family. These are particularly welcome because they bloom in late summer.

Space Invaders

In spite of its prettiness, because it is so invasive soapwort is not a good plant to introduce into a mixed border whether of herbs or of other kinds of garden plants. This is a fault with some other kinds.

Mints, for instance, are notorious in this respect. Where they have to be controlled, their roots are best restricted in some way. One old-fashioned but quite effective method is to plant the mint in a bottomless bucket sunk into the ground so that its rim is just above the soil to ensure that the roots cannot roam on the surface itself. Any other type of firm container with the same advantages will do for this purpose. On a patio or some other paved area, the practice of removing a paving stone to make a planting space will suit mints and keep them from roaming. They and others can also be grown in little island beds apart from other plants. Where space is scarce several varieties of mints and other invaders can be grown together. They can also be container-grown separately (see chapter two).

Horseradish, another space invader, would in the old days usually be confined to some area where it could be allowed to spread. This is a plant which grows readily from root cuttings, and since it is almost impossible to lift whole roots, portions which remain in the soil soon grow into new roots, so it does not take long for a colony to become established. In some gardens the area near a compost heap, or as in my own garden, near a bonfire site, could be used for this plant.

Decorative Foliage

Happily, many of the most useful herbs are of an evergreen nature, although their foliage may not actually be green. Lavender, thyme, rosemary and sage are examples. If these are generously planted in a utility herb border they will give it a well-furnished and interesting appearance in winter when the herbaceous kinds have died down. They have the advantage also of protecting the dormant plants. Where the boundaries of the border are to be well defined, es-

Above The striking colours of *Salvia officinalis* 'Tricolor' are a bonus to sage growers. The leaves, commonly used in soups and meat dishes, are strongly aromatic, and impart a distinctive, sharp flavour

Right Honeysuckle, a native plant in Britain and commonly known as woodbine, is cultivated for its delicate, drifting perfume which fills the air on summer evenings

pecially if a formal path runs along it, or if it is surrounded by paving, thyme can be used as a low edging. It should be kept regularly cut so that the plants remain low and neat.

At its peak, even a culinary herb border should look decorative, for there are many kinds of plants which have handsome foliage, fennel, both apple-green and bronze-leaved, sweet cicely, sage, balm and angelica for example. If potpourri herbs are to be included then the range widens and among others we can include artemisias, some of which are beautifully silver (there are enough of this family, incidentally, to form an interesting collection), santolina and the curry plant, *Helichrysum angustifolium*, curry scented only and not used in the preparation of curry powder. It is edible but bitter and best used in moth-repellent mixtures.

Those who like variegations or foliage colours other than green in plants will find that the culinary herbs offer many collectable varieties, all of which can be used in cooking in the same way as the plain-leaved species. There are, for instance, some ten or more varieties of

sage, *Salvia officinalis*. In the leaves of one variety, 'Tricolor', you may see beautiful splashes of magenta among the green and cream, and the purple sage, *S.o.* 'Purpurascens', is so handsome that park gardeners often use it in the brilliant bedding schemes they favour. Sages, like lavender, look lovely when planted in association with roses, both old and modern kinds. Golden marjoram is as bright as any flower and if you plant variegated balm where it is in full sunshine, it too will display itself vividly and contribute greatly to garden colour.

Flowering Herbs

The flowers of the culinary herbs are not all as flamboyant as the poppy and prolific as fennel. Many are inconspicuous: balm is an example, at least to us. Balm flowers are sought after eagerly by bees and others. However, massed and contrasted with care they can prove to be decorative enough.

Where the gardener would like to see more vividly coloured blooms among the leafy herbs, especially those kinds which can be cut for arrangement, there are several herbal kinds, annual, biennial and perennial; not all are suitable for cooking but they can be used for potpourri and similar purposes. Among these, to mention but a few, are the glorious poppies already mentioned, pot marigolds, borage and vivid blue alkanet, fragrant-leaved bergamot, yarrow — there is a beautiful rose-red variety — and bistort. If there is space enough in

the garden, other plants to choose from are the old-fashioned strongly scented roses, honeysuckle, jasmine, cistus, mock orange, wintersweet, elder, tutsan and mallow.

FORMAL HERB GARDENS

But what of the special herb gardens which some people wish to create? Gardens where the keynote is traditional formality and a certain amount of uniformity? Such a garden is best planned on paper and later on the ground before you begin to plant, for the actual design may need a great deal of thought beyond that of the visual concept.

Where it is the gardener's dream to create a knot garden with geometrically shaped beds, each neatly edged with, perhaps, thyme, dwarf lavender or hyssop, the paths which run between them are an important part of the design. These need not be very wide, but they should be wide enough to allow for traffic and for actual gardening. They can be surfaced in various ways, paved or gravelled. One such garden I knew as a child was paved with cockle shells. Alternatively they can be planted and covered with pennyroyal, carpeting thyme or chamomile, in which case they should be wide enough to take a mower.

So far as the plants which are grown within these formal edgings are concerned, there is a danger that if one sets out to grow only those plants which can be clipped so they are maintained at one level, usually a little higher than the edging, the gardener may find that the range may not be as wide as had been hoped and that many culinary herbs are excluded. Where it is hoped to include the tall plants such as fennel, lovage, sweet cicely, angelica, tarragon and apple mint, for instance, these need to be placed in such a way that their presence does not mar the symmetry of the overall design. For instance, where the garden is to fill a rectangular space, it may be that corner beds can be designed to take these plants, while the most uniform in size occupy the central space.

The herb wheel, a circular bed divided into segments representing the spaces between the spokes of a wheel, the spokes themselves being of clipped edging plants, is a design often put forward as being suitable. Certainly it can look very attractive on paper, but here again there are one or two drawbacks. Unless the wheel is small enough, there is difficulty both in gathering and clipping herbs near the centre. It is better to make the design large rather than small, ideally with paths running alongside the spokes and around the hub at the centre. Another drawback is that if the wheel pattern is chosen for appearance' sake alone, we are back with only the limited kinds which can be grown neatly, for once the plants which grow tall begin to do so, the overall spoke pattern is obscured. However, it *is* possible to keep most of the plants low so that the wheel pattern remains obvious. It is usually best, in any case, to alternate the herbs according to height, so that low growers are in one section, taller kinds next to them and so on. Where they are to be included, the very tallest can be stationed around the rim of the wheel. Mint, which has to be strictly confined, could be kept at the very centre.

Another pattern which appears to grip the imagination is that of a snail or helix. Here a continuous path between narrow borders gradually spirals to a central point, or vice-versa. This is a fun garden for those who have children in the family. It can be sited anywhere there is space for a circular bed, for in effect this is what it is. Should this have to fit into a rectangular plot, the corners thus created could be planted with flowering shrubs, bay or rosemary, or four different tall herbs, one for each corner.

In the main the same remarks apply. The gardener has to decide whether it is the visual effect or the convenience of the design which is of the greater importance. In many ways the snail border offers the gardener the most opportunities for imaginative gardening. Is it, for instance, planted in such a way that we are led through dwarf herbs gradually to taller and taller kinds until at the centre we find the tallest of all, with perhaps a clipped bay tree rising above them? Or are the tallest kinds planted all around the perimeter border, thus creating a 'secret garden' within? Obviously there are many variations which can be played on this theme and obviously also, so much depends upon the size of the snail! It has one thing in its favour for those who are likely to go on collecting herbs. So long as there exists sufficient space, the outer path can be extended to make one or more spirals around the existing outside.

THE HERB WHEEL *Below* This attractive formal design
may be planted up with a wide range of herbs – the
selection shown here is an example. Two kinds of
mint are confined to the hub at the centre

SNAIL PATTERN *Right* This imaginative design is great
fun to plant up. The shape is defined by a dwarf
hedge of lavender and the pattern is made more
colourful by the inclusion of various forms of balm,
sage and fennel. The pot in the centre may be used
for a bay tree or lemon verbena or sweet cicely

1 Chives
2 Balm
3 Basil
4 Fennel
5 Thyme
6 Parsley
7 Tarragon
8 Chervil
9 Sweet cicely
10 Marjoram
11 Rosemary
12 Winter savory
13 Sage
14 Lovage
15 Spearmint
16 Apple mint

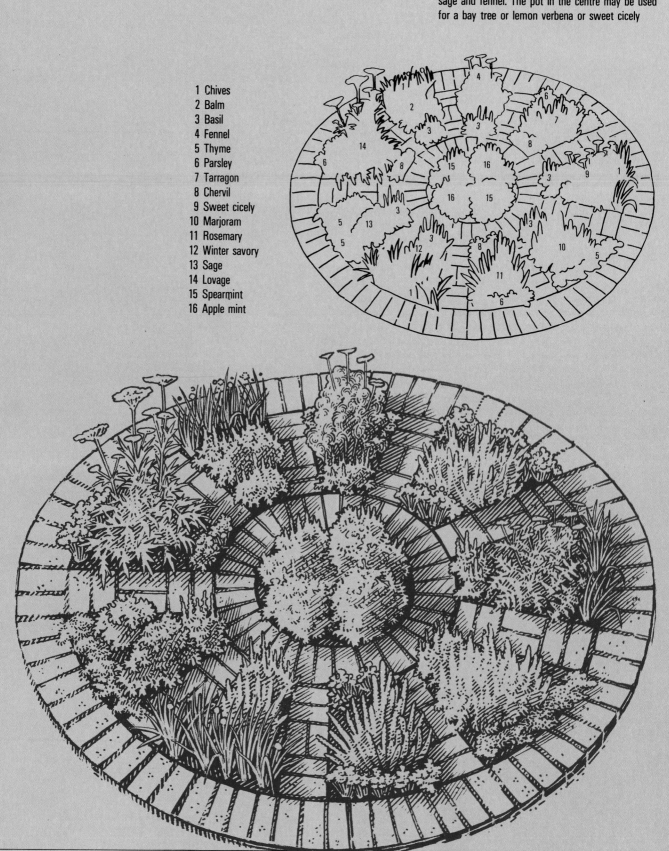

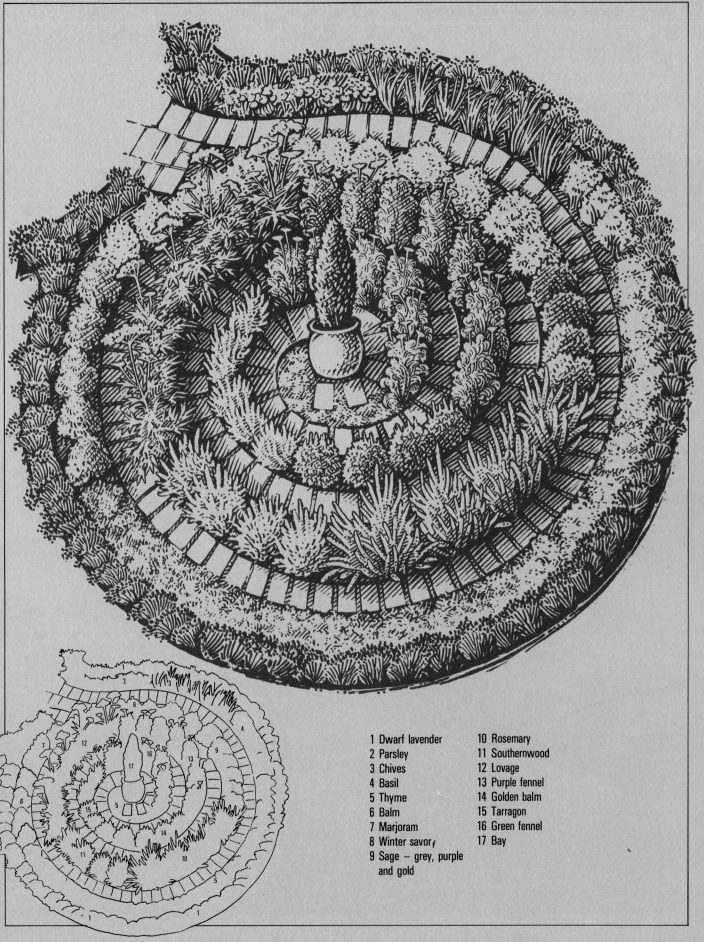

1 Dwarf lavender
2 Parsley
3 Chives
4 Basil
5 Thyme
6 Balm
7 Marjoram
8 Winter savory
9 Sage – grey, purple and gold

10 Rosemary
11 Southernwood
12 Lovage
13 Purple fennel
14 Golden balm
15 Tarragon
16 Green fennel
17 Bay

CHAPTER TWO

GROWING HERBS IN POTS

S OME OF THE evergreen, shrubby herbs, among them rosemary, lavender, sage, santolina, curry plant, southernwood and, of course, bay, can look delightful when grown in containers. Some of them can be clipped to be formal in appearance, while others can sprawl and be allowed to cascade prettily over the rims of the pots which hold them.

Containers of herbs are especially suited to paved areas, which may range from noble balustraded terraces to more humble patios linking the house with the garden proper. The containers, of course, should be chosen from the wide range available to suit their particular setting.

Below Herbs planted in a wooden trough, and *opposite*, in a fixed pottery tub. Herbs may be grown in a variety of containers, including old baths, milk churns, buckets, window boxes, teapots and saucepans, provided the soil is suitable and there is room for the roots to spread

Depth of Container

Most gardens are almost certain to have space to spare to grow those herbs that prefer more open and freer rooting conditions, plants such as fennel, parsley, lovage, mint and tarragon. But where there exists no real garden, where maybe there is only a tiny backyard, balcony, roof garden, space at the side of a path to the garage or the house, or perhaps simply a windowsill, even these deeper-rooting kinds, as well as many others, can be grown in containers. The important thing to bear in mind is that the deeper the container, or the more space for soil that it provides, the more root room there is for the plant and the greater the yield.

Window boxes, for instance, should never be less than 15–20cm (6–8in) deep. Where they are deeper than this, some herbs like thyme and marjoram, or rosemary and sage, which are best planted at each end of a mixed group, can be encouraged to trail over the edge attractively so that the boxes do not present bare and unattractive faces to the world.

Drainage

One reason why containers need to be deep is that ideally they should not be filled with compost from base to rim, space for watering should be left above the soil level and all kinds should be supplied with a layer of drainage material for about a quarter of their depth below the compost. Excess water can drain away naturally into this and thus keep the soil or compost aerated and free from waterlogging. Roots rot in persistently

Above An unglazed earthenware pot makes one of the most attractive holders for herbs. The natural hues of the container look especially good behind the fine, lacy fronds of plants such as thyme, parsley, caraway and sweet marjoram

wet soil, though not in a medium which is just pleasantly moist and contains some air. The drainage layer can consist of one kind of material or a mixture of crocks, for instance broken flower pots, other kinds of pottery, stones and charcoal.

The gardener has to strike a balance between providing the plants with adequate water, yet ensuring that the soil does not become waterlogged. A good drainage system helps considerably, so see also that there are suitable drainage holes in the base of the container, or at the sides near the base.

Watering

It is important to appreciate that probably the most critical factor in growing good plants in containers is watering. Where some herbs, particularly the shrubby exotics, might struggle on thirstily, apparently without damage, for a fairly long period, other kinds soon die if water is withheld even for a short time. Certainly their rate of growth will be affected. The softer and lusher the texture and nature of the herb, the more

dependent it is on adequate water supplies. It is sometimes difficult to assess the rate at which water is being lost. Although it can be seen flowing from the base of a container after watering or rainfall, it is also evaporating invisibly from the sides of the container and from the soil and plants themselves all the time, more so in hot weather — and sometimes to a surprising degree.

Take care if hoses are used for watering. A jet of water directed at a plant does little good, in fact stems and leaves can be bruised and broken this way. Whether using a hose or watering can, pour in the water gently, near the edge of the container. Allow it to fill to the brim.

On the other hand, provided a gentle touch is applied, herbs can be kept clean, healthy and attractive by spraying them with clean water, either with a hose or from the rose of a watering can. This may be necessary from late spring onwards until some time in the autumn, according to weather conditions. It is best to do this in early morning before the sun is shining brightly on the plants, and in the evening during spells of warm weather.

Feeding

After some weeks of successive waterings some of the plant foods may have become leached out of the soil. This is a reason why plants should be fed with a soluble general plant food from time to time. Hungry plants are not productive. Directions, regarding the method of application or rate of dilution, given on the fertiliser or plant food packet or bottle should be followed faithfully.

Potting Composts

Now, what of the soil itself? This must be good, which means that it should be both retentive of moisture yet porous and should contain the requisite plant foods. Simple soil lifted from the countryside or a garden is not suitable. Other ingredients, humus, peat and sand, for instance, need to be incorporated in order to create the rooting medium which will be accepted by the plants.

There are many kinds of rooting mediums on sale at garden stores and centres and known generally as potting composts. They are divided into those based on soil which has been sterilised in order to kill spores of fungi, insect pests and weed seeds, and those based on peat. The latter are light in weight, an important point for those who garden above ground level. They are also less likely to become waterlogged.

Soil in containers deteriorates after a while. That holding long-lived plants should be topdressed annually with new compost so that it becomes rejuvenated. To do this, simply scrape out with a trowel the top few centimeters (inch or two) of soil, being careful never to dig deeply or roughly enough to injure any roots. then top up with fresh soil to the old level. This is well worth doing because some herbs will live for years in one container if care is taken of them.

Don't hesitate to repot a herb from a small container to a larger one if it appears not to be growing as fast as it should.

Above A strawberry pot is a useful container for a mixed planting of herbs because it is large enough to hold a reasonable amount of compost. Fill the pot gradually with compost, planting up each pocket as the soil reaches that level, or, with small plants, fill the entire pot first and then position the plants

Left The pockets of the strawberry pot are scattered over its surface and so are useful for a selection of herbs where space is restricted

CHOOSING A CONTAINER

Deep, outsize, terracotta flower pots, tubs or similar vessels are best for those tall herbs with thongy roots, such as fennel, angelica and lovage. These are often best grown alone, but where a container is fairly wide in diameter at the top, as some imitation stone 'saucers' are, there is no reason why seeds of some smaller, shorter-lived herbs should not be sown in the surface soil near the container edge, basil and chervil for instance, both of which are easily pulled out when they are finished. It is best not to grow those which have to be dug out and cause disturbance to the main plant or plants.

The shrubby herbs appear to get along quite well together, so that it is possible to mix, say, thyme, rosemary and winter savory in one container, while in another a different kind of thyme, lemon thyme for instance, sage and an unclipped bay could be grown. These can prove useful if placed near the house to be conveniently at hand in winter.

The terracotta crocus pots or strawberry pots (they have pocket holes dispersed at intervals all over the surface) can also be used for herbs. Basil, summer savory and sweet marjoram grow well this way and an advantage in their case is that pots can be kept indoors, with the plants slowly maturing, until the weather is suitable for them to be stood outdoors.

This practice can also be adopted for some of the more permanent herbs, rosemary, sage and winter savory in particular, which can be potted singly but in conventional flower pots and treated as house plants in winter, at which time they will be conveniently near at hand, and stood outdoors from early summer until the frosts come. Give them good light. Light is much more important than heat in this case and this applies to all indoor-grown herbs.

Window Boxes

Tarragon is not really a good mixer and where possible is best grown alone. However, if space is scarce it can be grown in a window box with others. Treat it like mint and make a special division for it to keep its roots strictly in one place. A tile or a piece of thick black plastic cut to size, used inside the box and fitting across it snugly from one side to the other, should prove effective.

Other suitable perennial and shrubby plants for a window box are chives, marjoram and winter savory, plus the biennial parsley. There are also those kinds that are raised annually, either by seed sown in situ, such as chervil, or as in the case of basil, summer savory, sweet or knotted marjoram, raised as half-hardy annuals and transplanted when all danger of frosts has passed.

When the latter are to be mixed with the more permanent kinds, it helps to keep an empty flower pot 'planted' to mark the site. When ready to plant them, remove the empty pot and replace it with the contents of a full one of the same size, or with a single plant and a little extra compost. This way transplanting takes place without injury to neighbouring plants.

Hanging Baskets

Hanging baskets can be used for herbs. A parsley basket, which can be kept for two years if it is not allowed to flower, is a favourite, but be sure that it does not hang in full sun. Basil, summer savory and sweet marjoram, on the other hand, love the sun. Choose the type of basket which allows you to push seedlings through the wires or holes over the outer surface, and plant more in the top, of course. As the plants grow they will gradually cover the entire surface. The basket must be kept well watered, so hang it in a convenient place where drips will do no harm. For instance, have it suspended over a pot of herbs such as mint, which will benefit from the drips.

Right Parsley, with its long tap root, grows best in tall, cylindrical containers like the parsley pot shown here resting in a shallow watering bowl

Growing Herbs Indoors

It is possible to buy special packs of herbs recommended for growing on the kitchen windowsill. This can be done, but to expect one or two small pots to supply a cook for weeks on end is just not realistic. Think only, for instance, of how much parsley is needed to flavour and colour a white sauce, a good tablespoonful or more when finely chopped. This will take most of the leaves from a plant grown in a small pot. After these leaves have been cut there will be a considerable period before more have grown ready for use.

So obviously one pot of each herb is not sufficient if the supply is to be as continuous as possible, but with a little planning it should be possible for most indoor gardeners to produce a succession of small supplies of fresh herbs. Look for suitable space on other windowsills about the house or on tables near windows and/or in sheltered places outdoors. Here pots can be stood either to grow on while others are in use or to recuperate after being harvested. These can be moved around as necessary. The smallest number to aim for is three of a kind.

Three pots of chives should provide a succession of cutting material for the average cook. These are satisfactory plants to grow, possibly because the 'grass' lengthens so quickly after cutting, and it is necessary only to tip the stems rather than to cut them right down.

In some ways the same applies to mint, where the cook often requires just a sprig or two rather than a larger quantity. Use a terracotta pot rather than a plastic one for this herb and keep it standing in a little water in a saucer. The water will then be drawn up into the pottery in sufficient quantities to keep the soil moist. Mint can also be grown in a puddle pot, that is, in a watertight vessel filled with washed gravel or other stones, crocks, even broken household pottery, to anchor the roots, and a little charcoal to keep the water sweet. If you own special hyacinth glasses, fill these with mint roots once the bulbs are spent.

It is usual to lift mint from the garden in order to grow it this way. Chives, too, can be treated this way, but this herb can also be raised quite easily from seed, even treated as an annual should this prove to be most convenient. This applies also to some perennial herbs — fennel and dill — which would normally

be much too big and untidy at maturity for indoor cultivation.

Usually though, it is many of the annuals which are most often grown in pots indoors and details of cultivation are given in the following chapter. There is also a simple method of growing in which the young plants are regarded as expendable. This is to sow several pots of one kind of herb in succession, say two at daily intervals. As soon as the seedlings are worth using — a point to be determined by tasting them for pungency — cut them right down to soil level and use these tops. Then pull up the roots, clean the surface, add a little new compost and re-sow with the same kind. Put that pot to the back of the queue and move on to the next one that is ready.

Indoor herb gardening need not be confined to those who have no gardens. Many plants can be lifted in autumn and grown on in the warmth of the house in late autumn, winter and early spring. Mint, chives, tarragon, fennel and parsley are examples. More of this in the following chapter.

Above Herbs such as chives, parsley and mint may be grown inside, on windowsills or in the greenhouse. A number of pots of each kind of herb will provide a continuous supply for the harvest of stems and leaves

CHAPTER THREE

CULTIVATION

Opposite Sage, thyme and marjoram sown in quantities large enough to ensure good pickings throughout the summer season

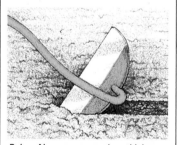

Below Sowing seed out of doors. First take out a shallow drill with the corner of a hoe or rake

Below Always sow seed as thinly as possible. Cover lightly with a layer of soil and then water

M OST HERBS CAN be easily grown from seed. There are various methods used according to the nature of the plant itself and where it is to be raised.

SOWING OUTDOORS

Those kinds which are to be grown in rows, say in the kitchen garden, are usually hardy annuals or, like parsley, mainly treated as such. These are sown in drills, or shallow channels, drawn out with the corner of a hoe, using a garden line stretched across the plot as a guide. Sometimes when short drills are to be drawn a rake or hoe handle is used instead of a line.

It is important that the seed is sown both thinly and at a shallow depth, just deep enough for it to be lightly covered when the drill is filled in again. This is usually done by pushing the raised soil back into the drill with the back of the up-turned rake.

Growing the seed thinly ensures that there is less thinning of seedlings to be done later. It also means that the emergent seedlings do not have to struggle quite so fiercely with their fellows for living space. The thinnings are best discarded, unless, of course, they are large enough to be used as flavouring.

Seeds can be shaken from the packet into the drill, but inexpertly done this sometimes results in uneven sowing. It is easier and more convenient first to empty some seed into a small dish and then to take it up a pinch at a time. This way it can be thinly sprinkled into the drill. The nearer you are to the drill the easier it is to control the distribution of the seed.

When seeds of annuals or biennials are to be sown in a herb border between more permanent plants they can be broadcast evenly all over the space provided, or alternatively sown in shallow circular drills, easily made by running the tip of a trowel, cane or dibber around the outside of the rim of an upturned flower pot or bucket. As the plants grow they gradually fill the space in the centre. See that sufficient empty ground exists on the outside of the circle when the drill is to be made so that the plants can extend in that direction also.

Soil

The soil for herbs should always be well prepared, that is, previously well dug so that it is open and well drained, and enriched with compost, animal manure or some all-round fertiliser, organic for preference. Obviously it should be clear of weeds. Before sowing it should be raked until a good fine tilth is formed.

If the space in which the seeds are to be sown is a small one and not easily treated with a rake, prepare the surface by using a small handfork, scratching the surface back and forth until it is level and free of all clods.

Sowing Times

Some seeds require a higher temperature than others before they will germinate. Some, the half-hardy annuals for instance, need to be sown 'in heat' in order to give them a longer growing season. This means raising the seedlings in a greenhouse, in a special propagating case or perhaps on the windowsill of a

Above An outdoor sowing of the common curly leaved and the flat, broad leaved varieties of parsley. A biennial plant, its flower stalks should be removed in the second year to prevent it going to seed

warm room. The seed of these half-hardies can be sown outdoors in early summer, but there is the likelihood that they may not produce a crop. In cool summers the plants are long in maturing and seldom lush. It is best where possible to sow both indoors and out and to plant out the heat-raised kinds, such as basil and sweet marjoram, in early summer.

So far as hardy annuals are concerned it is sometimes prudent in spring to delay their sowing until you judge the soil to be warm enough. This applies even if custom dictates that they should be sown at an earlier date. Soil can be dried and warmed up in advance by covering an area with cloches for a few days before the proposed sowing date.

Hardy annual seed is sown at two seasons of the year, in late summer or early autumn, while the soil is still warm, or in spring as it begins to warm up. Where there is sufficient garden space to spare it is a good plan to sow some seed at both seasons to extend their period of use. Autumn-sown plants mature earlier than those sown in spring, but should there be a hard winter some of the seedlings may not survive and so the gardener may need to supplement them by a spring sowing and thus ensure a sufficiency of plants.

Germination

Many of the umbellifers, (members of the family *Umbelliferae*), parsley and angelica in particular, produce seed which soon loses its viability, so is best sown after ripening.

If it is not to be wasted, one way of making sure that seed is viable is to sow an experimental pinch in a pot indoors. If it germinates readily it can be grown with confidence in the way intended.

Sometimes, and especially again where the parsley family is concerned, germination is prolonged. Parsley is notoriously slow and can even take as long as eight weeks to appear. Often too-deep sowing is the cause of poor or tardy growth. It is helpful to mark the spot where parsley is sown by sowing some radish seed in the same place. To do this after the parsley seed has been sown, go back along the drill and thinly scatter radish seed among the parsley. Fill in the drill. The radish, which both germinates and matures quickly, should be ready to pull by the time the parsley seedlings appear. Parsley seed sown twice a year ensures a steady supply.

Self-seeding

In my own garden chervil is allowed to seed itself. Consequently it appears very early in the year when fresh green herbs are especially welcome. It is often in flower by April. But not all gardeners have the space to allow plants to seed themselves. Furthermore, self-seeding is a chancy business and not to be relied upon. To be sure of a good crop of herbs, it is necessary to sow seed or to divide roots or take cuttings, according to the herb in question.

SOWING SEED INDOORS

If you hope to grow herbs indoors and are buying new pots, choose the squat, wide kind rather than those that are taller and more tapering. Small pots, 10–15cm (4–6in) in diameter, are most suitable for windowsill gardening and useful for raising seed.

Seedlings should be given a good start in life and encouraged to grow quickly. They do better if they are grown in a specially prepared seed compost and there are many good brands on sale.

season and where they are to grow, they can either be planted out in the garden or potted individually.

Alternatively, as soon as they can be handled they can be transferred individually to separate pots. This is the best method in many ways, not least because little disturbance is caused to the roots of the plants. Begin by using quite small pots. As the herbs grow and their roots fill these, move them on to a slightly larger size and so on until it is time to plant them out, or if they are to be pot-grown, until they have reached the ultimate size.

Fill the pot with seed compost to within at least 1cm (½in) of the rim, water it and allow it to drain. Sow the seed thinly all over the surface and cover with a very fine layer of compost. Slip the entire pot into a transparent plastic bag. Inflate this and close the top. The pot is now in its own little greenhouse where the temperature will remain even and water will be prevented from evaporating from the compost. Remove the pot from the bag as soon as the seed leaves appear.

Pricking Out

Although a seed compost provides for the needs of the newly emerging plants, it does not contain sufficient food for them to continue to grow well. A stronger growing medium is needed along with more space for each plant. Seedlings are best moved into a potting compost as soon as they are large enough to handle. At this point they can be 'picked off' or 'pricked out' into seed-boxes, set 2cm (¾in) or so apart each way. There they can stay until they touch, at which point, according to the

Potting On

To transplant from one pot to another, first make sure that the soil has been watered. With fingers outstretched over the pot's rim and on each side of the plant or plants to prevent them and the soil from falling, turn the pot upside down. Tap its rim against a table edge or some other solid surface so that the complete rootball comes out cleanly into your hand. Have some compost ready in a larger pot and sit the rootball on this, making sure that the layer of compost is deep enough to lift the plant up to its original level. Fill the space around the rootball with more compost and firm this down well. Water and allow to drain.

If instead of one plant the pot contains several seedlings which are to be pricked out or potted, lay the rootball on the table and gently separate the seedlings, taking care to damage their roots as little as possible. As each one is separated from the rest, pot it, water it in and leave it to drain. After transplanting, always keep the plants out of direct sunlight for two or three days.

Top left Sow seed indoors by sprinkling it thinly on a pot of seed compost. Make sure the surface of the compost is level and slightly firmed

Bottom far left Place the pot in a plastic bag. Inflate this and tie the top, then keep it away from direct sunlight. Remove the pot from the bag as soon as the seedlings germinate

Bottom left Once seedlings are large enough to handle, they should be moved to another pot or box to give them more space. Take care not to damage the fragile stems when moving the seedlings

Right Pot on plants as soon as the roots have filled the existing pot. When doing this, make sure the plant is at its original level in the new pot by placing a layer of compost under it. Trickle compost around the rootball, firm with the fingers and then water well

If the plants are eventually to be grown outside, once they are growing well they should be 'hardened off'. That is, they should be stood outside whenever the weather is mild, but they should be kept under cover and away from possible frost at nights.

During this time turn the pot upside down occasionally to keep an eye on the roots. If these begin to wander from the drainage holes, take it as a sign that the plant needs more food. Either plant it in the garden if conditions are right, or move it on to a slightly larger pot.

This applies also to individual plants grown indoors.

Pot-grown Herbs

Pricking out and transplanting is not necessary for those indoor herbs which are to be cut as soon as they are of a useful size and then discarded. In their case, to ensure that they will receive enough food while remaining in the pot in which they were sown, fill it first with potting compost, leaving sufficient space, about 2–3cm (¾–1¼in), for a top layer of seed compost. Follow the directions for seed sowing given above. As the seedlings grow and their roots travel down the pot they will come into contact with the richer soil.

Watering

Always keep pot plants in good light. See that the compost never dries out completely yet that it does not become waterlogged. The safest method is to allow the compost to become almost dry and then to water it thoroughly, filling the pot with water to the brim. Allow the water to run through the compost to a saucer below. Give it an hour to take back up what water is needed and after this time empty away any water remaining in the saucer.

SOWING PERENNIAL HERBS

Seed for perennial herbaceous plants and shrubby herbs can be sown outdoors, usually in a specially prepared plot of ground or a nursery bed, but most gardeners find it more satisfactory to sow the seed in pots or boxes in the way described above and then gradually to harden the seedlings off and plant them outdoors. If they are sown outside remember to transplant them from the seed row or patch as soon as possible. Bear in mind that by moving plants two or three times when they are young, you encourage them to develop a good mass of fibrous roots. Usually for the first transplanting the seedlings are spaced about 5–8cm (2–3in) apart.

When their leaves touch they are lifted and transplanted again with more space between each one. Plants left crowded in a row tend to develop tough or stringy tap roots and on lifting these often get broken. Even if unbroken, because they are tough they have some difficulty in adapting to the move. A ball of smaller, more fibrous roots usually settles down quickly, which means that the plant it supports suffers less of a check.

DIVIDING HERBS

A young herbaceous plant has one well defined centre. As it grows older it may develop several shoots around the original, gradually growing into a clump. Sometimes this grows much too large or becomes bare and unproductive in parts. Most long-lived perennials are rejuvenated, and propagated at the same time, by division, which is best done when the plants are resting, from autumn until spring.

First cut down the current year's stems and then lift the clump with a fork. Some plants can be pulled apart with the hands quite easily, tearing them into several sections, some small with only one shoot and others larger, according to requirements.

Tough, compacted plants may need to be prised apart. The usual method is to use two garden forks plunged into the mass back to back. The forks are then forced apart, thus separating the roots into at least two portions. This is easiest to do with two long-handled forks, but failing this equipment use a digging fork and a hand fork. The levering action should split the plant in two, or divide it sufficiently for it then to be pulled apart. These two sections can be divided further using the same method. Discard old pieces of both plant and root. Select the best of the divided pieces and replant these in the herb garden or the nursery bed for future use. Bear in mind that some can be potted for indoor cultivation in the winter.

Plants with thongy roots are simply propagated by lifting a stem or a group of stems with a root portion attached, which may have to be cut away from the main mass. This can be done at almost any time for mint, but is best done in autumn and spring for tarragon.

As a rule the shrubby herbs are not easily divided, but thyme is an exception. Pull a plant apart in such a way that each division has some root attached. The rooted pieces can be planted directly in the garden but they should be kept watered if the weather is dry.

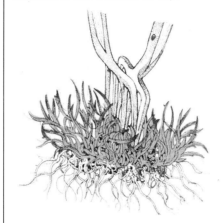

TAKING CUTTINGS

The shrubby herbs are best propagated by seed or heel cuttings. These cuttings are taken in early or late summer, a 8–10cm (3–4in) piece of shoot being pulled away from the stem in such a way that a small piece of bark comes with it. This is trimmed cleanly and the cutting inserted into the rooting medium. An excellent method is to prepare a little plot in semi-shade just large enough to be covered by a cloche. Spread a layer of clean horticultural sand over the soil surface. Prepare the cuttings and dibble them into this. Water them, allow the foliage to dry and then cover them. Keep them covered until the spring. On a smaller scale use a flower pot enclosed in a transparent plastic bag.

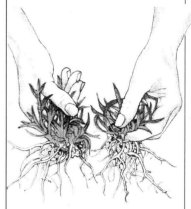

Below Large clumps of perennial herbs can be rejuvenated by division. Do this with two garden forks and then pull the pieces apart with the hands

Above Mint is easily propagated by lifting pieces of the root, cutting this into sections and either planting these in a new site or potting them up as shown

Below To make a heel cutting, pull a piece of shoot away from the main stem and then trim the small piece of bark that comes with it. Insert in a pot of compost

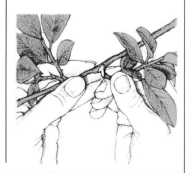

CHAPTER FOUR

HARVESTING, DRYING AND PRESERVING

Opposite Dry bunches of herbs awaiting crushing and grinding with mortar and pestle for later use in the kitchen

Right Herbs gathered fresh from the garden, just before flowering, have high levels of oils which give them a strong flavour

For CENTURIES HERBS have been harvested and either dried or preserved in some way so that their scents, flavours and other qualities can be captured and released later in foods or medicine, ointments and lotions, or in potpourri, salves, creams and other sweet-smelling products.

It is the essential oils present in most herbs, particularly in the culinary kinds, which give each of them its characteristic scent and/or flavour. When the parts of the plants are dried they shrink, yet their oil content remains much the same. In cooking, this quite often means that a pinch of a dried herb is usually sufficient to take the place of, say, a heaped tablespoon of the same herb when fresh. But except for bay leaves, herbs are best used freshly gathered.

Where there are plenty of the shrubby herbs growing in the garden, thyme, rosemary and sage for example, it should not be necessary to dry them for kitchen use, for they can be gathered throughout the winter. However, even these particular culinary kinds have their uses in health and beauty products.

Not all culinary herbs dry well. They fail to retain their pungency once they have lost their freshness. This applies especially to the herbaceous kinds with succulent leaves — balm, borage and chives for instance. However, fennel, parsley, mint and chervil dry well and although not quite so fully flavoured as when they are fresh, they make a good substitute.

It is helpful to keep a posy of fresh herbs near at hand in a kitchen. Gathered

Right Freezing is an excellent method of preserving soft leaved herbs like mint, sage, nasturtium and dandelion, as well as those with needle-like leaves such as juniper and rosemary. For long term storage it is advisable to blanch herbs by dipping them in boiling water and then cold water before packing them into freezer bags

and treated like cut flowers, that is, stem ends stripped so that no leaves are under water, and stood in clean water in a clean vessel, herbs should keep in good condition for several days if placed in strong daylight but not in direct sun.

STORING IN THE REFRIGERATOR

Alternatively they can be kept in a refrigerator. In this case wash them first if necessary, dry them gently on kitchen paper without bruising and when quite dry slip them into a plastic bag or canister.

Fresh herbs can also be deep frozen, either alone or partly prepared. For example, mint can be chopped with added sugar and packed in cartons ready for sauce. Chives can be chopped and mixed with a little white stock, ready for soup. Fish herbs, fennel, thyme and lovage, can be frozen in a little bouillon ready for use later for poaching the fish or making sauces. It is well worth experimenting in this way.

The leafy herbs such as chervil, coriander, fennel and parsley, can be frozen soon after cutting. Pack them in suitable quantities, one stem flat on another, and then either wrap them tightly in kitchen foil or put them in freezer bags. When ready for use they can either be used whole, tossed into the dish in preparation, or if they are to be fragmented, grated or shaved while they are still frozen.

HARVESTING HERBS

There are many other methods of preserving the characteristic herb flavours, all of which will be discussed in chapter six. These particular kinds should be dried while the leaves are still young, but old enough to be flavoursome. Most other herbs, the shrubby kinds, are best harvested just before they come into full bloom, for it is at this point that they contain the greatest quantity of their essential oils and consequently are most pungent.

Cut them on a dry, sunny day, using secateurs to make a clean cut. It is easy to damage a plant by trying to pick tough stems, such as those produced by thyme and other shrubby herbs. In most cases it is best to take the fuller portion at the tip of the stem rather than the whole stem, which becomes woodier and sparser towards its base. Usually the stems have to be separated from the foliage later if the herbs are powdered.

Make harvesting also a time to trim the shrubby herbs, cutting weak shoots away from the plant and generally making it more compact, particularly if it threatens to become too spreading. Once this is done new shoots should soon be produced.

It is wise to wash the culinary herbs in cold water before drying them, for they may have become splashed with mud, or be dusty or unclean in some other way. Swish them around in plenty of water either as loose stems or in small bunches.

Avoid squeezing or wringing them, for this bruises them and so releases the very oils you are is hoping to preserve. Shake the water from them and spread them out on a cloth or spin them in a salad drier to drain before preparing to dry them permanently.

TECHNIQUES FOR DRYING HERBS

If the herbs are to be bunched and hung to dry, see that they are in small bunches so that the air can circulate around them: about twelve stems to a bunch is a good number.

Oven Drying

There are several methods used for drying herbs. Possibly the most con-venient for most people is to hang them somewhere in the kitchen away from steam. The bunches can also be strung on sticks, or from the oven racks and left hanging in a cooling oven. Alternatively, they can be spread out on the oven racks, when they should be turned frequently. They can also be hung or spread out in an airing cupboard. Another good method is to hang them outdoors in half shade during the hottest part of the day. Be careful not to subject them to too much heat, for this will dry out the very volatile oils. Incidentally, this is one reason why the herb garden is so strongly scented on a very hot day.

The exceptions to this rule are the soft-leaved herbs, chervil, fennel, mint and parsley for instance, and it is worth experimenting with others which may not be listed here. These need a drying temperature of about 33–38°C (90–100°F) when they are oven-dried. They can be spread on kitchen foil and

Below Sprigs of herbs may be slowly dried by hanging them upside down in an airy place free of condensation where sunlight will not dissipate the oils or discolour the leaves

Above The dried parsley is placed in this glass jar to test for any remaining moisture which will be apparent on the sides of the container. For storage, dark, opaque containers are more suitable than transparent jars, because they block out the light which could damage the herbs

should be turned frequently so that the moisture is allowed to escape easily. This method can sometimes take several hours, depending on the lushness of the leaves, and this often depends in turn upon the season.

Air Drying

The quantities of the herbs to be dried largely determine the manner of drying. It is often much more convenient, and certainly simpler, to dry a few stems daily while the plants are at their best. To do this, pick a few stems, or in the case of fennel and similar herbs, leaves, wash them if necessary, and spread them, well spaced, on a piece of kitchen paper laid on a sunny windowsill in direct sunlight. If possible follow the sun around, moving the herbs from one windowsill to another. Once the herbs are brittle they

can be rubbed between the fingers to a powder, or alternatively pounded in a mortar or ground in a food processor or coffee grinder. If it is more convenient to powder a quantity rather than a few stems at a time, place the whole stems in an airtight jar to wait while others are being dried. Do not leave them lying around in the open. The dried shoots are inclined to absorb moisture from the air once humidity is present.

While it is not recommended that flowers, those gathered for potpourri for instance, should be dried in the sun because this is likely to cause their colours to fade, this method of drying herbs appears to have little effect on their colour, possibly because they dry so quickly. It is a most successful way of drying mint sprigs. In winter when these are boiled with potatoes or frozen peas the pungent steam fills the kitchen with the scent of summer.

Leaves which are to be used for tisanes and for potpourri mixtures and other products can be dried in the same way as described above. These are discussed in greater detail in chapter seven.

Drying Flowers

Old recipes for potpourri suggest that the flowers or petals are gathered on warm days and spread on linen laid on the ground in a shady place. This can be a nuisance should a breeze arise! A less arduous method is to hang the petals and flowers in an air current in net bags, the type used for packing fruits and vegetables. These are of various sized mesh, which means that it is possible to find a suitable grade for small flowers as well as larger kinds. It is important that air should circulate freely, so never completely fill the net bag. Instead pack it loosely and from time to time give the bags a shake so that the contents are moved around, those items in the centre being pushed to the outside. Also, if the drying seems to be prolonged, tip the contents of one bag into a fresh one so that the bottom petals are brought to the top. Once they feel dry, bring them into a dry place indoors. Store them in airtight jars ready for use.

Traditionally, the advice is that all scented flowers should be picked in their prime in order to preserve the strongest scent, and this is correct in the main. However, in some cases older petals have a stronger scent and in one case at least, that of roses, sometimes a flower which has no scent when fresh is sweetly scented when its petals are old and dried. Obviously it is worth experimenting. Rather than rob my garden of its fresh roses, I save all the petals from roses used in flower arrangements. The same applies to marigolds and any other scented daisies. These are dried and used in potpourri mixtures which are always delightfully scented when finally blended.

PRESERVING HERB ROOTS

Make use of edible herb roots. These are usually very full flavoured, or in the case of angelica and sweet cicely, sweet and scented. Scrub rather than peel them so that most of the pungency is retained.

Thick, thongy kinds can be powdered.

Wash them well, cut crosswise into sections and divide again should the root be more than 1cm (½in) or so thick. Spread them out on cooking foil. Dry them in a cool oven, an airing cupboard or on a shelf over a night storage heater or a radiator. Turn or stir frequently. When they are quite dry, pound them or (more easily) grind them to a powder. I use a coffee grinder for this purpose, having first wiped around the interior of the grinder with lemon juice to remove the coffee aroma. Alternatively, to remove the coffee smell, grind some of the herb's leaves or fresh stems first. Wipe the container quite dry before putting in the root. Store the powdered root in a screw-top jar.

Below Horseradish is harvested mainly for its roots. Like angelica and sweet cicely roots they can be dried but the process is tricky, the danger being a loss of pungency once the water content has been dispelled

CHAPTER FIVE

AN A TO Z OF
FAVOURITE HERBS

Opposite Chives make decorative as well as edible herbaceous plants

Right In botanical terms garlic is a vegetable, not a herb. It is used widely, however, for medicinal and culinary purposes. Reputed to reduce high blood pressure and aid digestion, it may be included in vinegars, oils and sauces, besides meat, cheese and fish dishes

OVER FIFTY HERBS are described in this chapter. All the most popular kinds are included together with some that are more unusual and well worth collecting. A description of the plant is followed by cultivation details, including propagation, and a guide to the uses that can be made of each particular herb.

The plants are listed in botanical name order with the common name following.

Allium sativum
GARLIC

A perennial, hardy bulb divided into 8 to 16 segments known as cloves, each segment or bulblet sheathed in a papery white cover. The flat, solid leaves grow to about 30cm (12in), sometimes with a flower stalk that terminates in an umbel of small white or pink flowers.

CULTIVATION Individual cloves should be planted in early spring in well cultivated soil in full sun. Plant about 2–3cm (¾–1¼in) deep and about 20cm (8in) apart in rows 30cm (12in) apart.

They usually grow well and easily and bulbs can be harvested in late summer when the foliage has yellowed and begun to die down. If left too long the entire bulb is apt to split and separate, making collection more difficult. Tie compound bulbs into the familiar rope shape, hang up in a cool, dry place and pull off single cloves for use in the kitchen as these are required.

USES One of the most ancient of herbs, originating in the deserts of the Middle East, garlic has been known and used for thousands of years both as a flavouring and as an antiseptic and medicine. It is no mere accident that it is used so widely in Asian, Indian, Chinese and even Mediterranean dishes, where typhus, cholera and similar infections were once common.

Because of its strength and pungency many objections have been raised to the use of garlic in cookery, although many who object to it consume it unknowingly and with pleasure, for if employed delicately in sensible quantities, it adds an individual and delicious flavour and aroma to many dishes from roasts and stews to salads. Some cooks merely rub the salad bowl with a clove, enough to introduce a subtle hint of ephemeral flavour. Certainly where complete cloves have been cooked with a stew, ragout or similar dish, they must be located and removed before serving to prevent them being eaten.

Allium schoenoprasum
CHIVES

Hardy perennial members of the lily family, chives grow from very small, flat

Right Dill is a herb which grows wild in the Mediterranean. In the garden it should be grown away from fennel, which it resembles, to avoid cross-pollination. Seed heads picked just before they are fully ripe give the best flavour

bulbs, producing quantities of thin, grass-like stems which are hollow and grow to about 15–30cm (6–12in). Plants produce many purple-pink pompons of pretty, nectar-rich flowers in summer.

CULTIVATION Chives can be grown from seed sown in spring or by dividing the grass-like clumps in autumn. They need sun and a good, rich, well-drained soil. They are greedy plants and should be kept well fed and never allowed to become dry if they are to perform well. Flowers can be used in salads, otherwise pinch them out to maintain growth of foliage unless the plants are required to play a decorative role, perhaps as an edging to a border.

Chives can be grown indoors in pots and forced into early leaf, but it should be borne in mind that a whole plant can be used for a single dish, so several pots will normally be required. The 'grass' will grow again when cut. Plants die down in winter.

USES Chives are the most delicious and the most delicately flavoured of the onions. Their bright green colour adds to the eye appeal of any dish in which they are used. They are normally cut finely with kitchen scissors and added as a garnish to soups, salads and in egg and cheese dishes. They can be blended with butters and soft cheeses and then refrigerator-stored. They can be dried and freeze-dried. Small quantities can be sealed fresh in plastic bags or boxes and kept crisp for several days in a refrigerator.

Aloysia triphylla
LEMON VERBENA

A deciduous shrub that will grow to 3m (10ft) or so in a warm, sheltered position, with long, lanceolate, pale green leaves, growing in threes, and somewhat insignificant lilac flowers. It came originally from South America and in cold districts here needs some winter protection. It is often potted up and brought under cover for the winter. Lemon verbena was previously called *Lippia citriodora*.

CULTIVATION A somewhat dry and arid soil helps keep lemon verbena plants sturdy, where a richer, moister medium might result in soft, lush but weak growth. Protect the plant in winter by cutting it down and covering the roots with straw. Propagate by taking softwood or heel cuttings in summer.

USES Lemon verbena leaves really do smell of lemon and this quality can be exploited by using them whenever and wherever lemon might otherwise be used. The leaves should be harvested when the flowers come into bloom and after drying should be stored in airtight containers, where they will keep their special fragrance even for years. Chopped or crushed leaves are used as a flavouring for some fish dishes and as an aromatic ingredient in jams and jellies. The long-lasting fragrance is particularly useful when the leaves are added to pot-pourri ingredients.

Anethum graveolens
DILL

A hardy annual which will reach up to 1m (3ft) in height, with dainty, loose umbels of little yellow flowers and thread- or string-like, bluish green foliage. It is an ancient plant, long cultivated and used by cooks and apothecaries because of its delicate, subtle flavour, so delicate in fact that it tends to disappear if cooked for too long, a waste that can be avoided by adding the herb to the dish at the last moment. Dill seeds, three-ribbed and dark brown, are as useful as the leaves, and have a slightly stronger, more bitter, though not unpleasant, flavour.

CULTIVATION Seed should be sown where the plants are to grow and the seedlings thinned to about 15cm (6in) apart. They usually require some sort of support, such as surrounding them, like peas, with twiggy sticks through which they can grow. If plants are allowed to become too dry in time of drought, or if their roots are disturbed or an attempt is made to transplant them, they tend to bolt and run quickly to seed. Dill leaves are so insubstantial and meagre that considerable quantities are necessary if they are to be dried. Whole flowers and seed heads are most often used in place of leaves alone for flavouring.

USES Dill is particularly suited to fish dishes of almost all kinds. It goes well also with salads and some of the more bland vegetables such as potatoes. Dill vinegar and dill pickles are well known and the herb seems to bring out a deeper flavour in cucumber. Gripe water or dill water was once used widely to comfort babies.

Angelica archangelica
ANGELICA

A striking, tall (1–2m/3–6ft), majestic herbaceous perennial, angelica is usually treated as a biennial because it normally dies after it has flowered in its second year. It sometimes takes four or five years for a plant to grow to maturity and to flower. If the flowers are removed the plant usually lives on. A typical member of the *Umbelliferae*, the plant has large leaves divided into toothed segments and the many greenish white flowers are held in a ball about 10–15cm (4–6in) across and produced in summer.

CULTIVATION Grow angelica from seed, but take care for this quickly loses its viability and is best sown as soon as it is ripe in early autumn. Choose a lightly shaded position in moist soil. It will seed itself naturally and, as the plant is relatively large, seedlings are best transplanted a little distance away from the parent plant.

USES Best known today as candied cake decoration, angelica is usually bought ready-made because of the lengthy process necessary to candy it, normally taking up to ten days. Leaf stems and midribs can be eaten. The roots also are edible and can be served as a vegetable. All parts of the plant are fragrant. The roots can be dried then ground or powdered like orris root to use as a fixative in potpourri (see page 82). The dried leaves, flowers and seeds can be used in potpourri and sweet bags. The great globular flowers can be dried for winter decoration. For this purpose allow them to make seed but cut them before this matures.

Left Cultivated for its ridged stems which may be candied, angelica's leaves are also valuable. Collected in early summer they may be infused in boiling water for a tisane or skin tonic, or used to flavour wines and fruit juices

Anthemis nobilis
CHAMOMILE

A low-growing, creeping, branched perennial about 15–20cm (6–8in) tall. There are two forms, single and double flowered and although both are suitable for making tea, the double form mainly is to be found on sale. The plant grows best in fairly dry, light but rich soil. It is good for seaside gardens where it can be used as a lawn. For this purpose a non-flowering form, *A.n.* 'Treneague' is adopted, although the common kind can also be used. Such lawns withstand much treading and should be mown regularly. Plants can be grown alone or mixed with grass. Botanically, chamomile has alternative names, *Matricaria chamomilla and Chamaemelum nobile.*

CULTIVATION To make a chamomile lawn, level, clear and enrich the soil with compost or an organic fertilizer to give young plants a good start. In spring tease the little plants apart and place at 15cm (6in) intervals over the area, planting firmly to avoid bird disturbance. Plants will very quickly spread and meet. Cut gently with shears to prevent flowers forming in the earlier weeks, but once roots are well established a mower with the blades set high may be used. If you wish to grow your own plants, broadcast seed in a special nursery bed and use the young plants for your lawn when they are large enough to handle safely.

USES *Anthemis nobilis* is suitable for little but a lawn and the non-flowering form is best for that. The plant was once highly valued as a febrifuge and tonic as well as for infusing in water as a rinse for blonde hair.

Chamomile

Anthriscus cerefolium
CHERVIL

A small, aromatic, slightly aniseed-flavoured annual herb, chervil is a vital fresh ingredient in many of the fine dishes of the gourmet. It grows to about 30cm (12in), has finely divided foliage and small white flowers gathered in umbels. All parts of the plant can be used, flowers, leaves, stems and root. The flavour is slightly reminiscent of caraway. Once established it self-seeds freely, a valuable quality as self-seeded plants are ready to pick in early spring.

CULTIVATION A good loam, fairly rich, in light shade is best for the cultivation of chervil. Sow the seeds in shallow drills and only just cover them with soil. They will germinate very quickly. Make sure the site is always kept moist. Seed can be sown in succession. Sow lightly in mid- to late spring for summer supplies and in late summer for winter. When the grass-like seed leaves appear thin out to about 25cm (10in) apart. The seedlings do not transplant well.

USES The keen and interested cook will make use of considerable quantities of chervil and may not find it easy always to obtain it in this country, so if possible a fair proportion of the kitchen garden should be allocated to it. This is one of the herbs that has greater culinary value than medical and is incomparably better fresh than dried. It is more widely used in continental Europe than in Britain, possibly because it appeared to originate there. It also has religious connotations, being known as one of the Lenten herbs and used widely on Maundy Thursday as a soup. Although aromatic and slightly sweet, it is not an aggressive herb and if too much is added to a dish it does not ruin the whole.

Artemisia abrotanum
SOUTHERNWOOD, LAD'S LOVE

A large genus of annuals, herbaceous perennials and shrubs, of which this, and the following three, are the most important herbs.

A hardy, fragrant shrub growing to 90cm (3ft) or so, with a tough, woody framework and slim, feathery, grey-green foliage. It seldom flowers, but in a

Left The fern-like leaves of chervil, ready to pick six weeks after sowing, can be harvested until the flowers bloom. They are generally added to soups, sauces, cream cheese, and fish and egg dishes

good summer spikes of small, brownish yellow blooms may appear in late summer.

CULTIVATION Grow in a light soil in full sun. Propagate by cuttings, softwood ones in early summer and heel ones in autumn.

USES Southernwood leaves are slightly bitter and have a taste and perfume reminiscent of lemons. Infusions are said to be a tonic and a stimulant. They used to be prescribed for nervous diseases and for 'female complaints'. Nowadays leaves are most often dried and used in potpourri as well as employed as a moth repellent, as the French name for the plant, *garde-robe*, suggests. The name lad's love has descended from the habit of using a sprig or two in a lover's bouquet as a symbol of faithful affection even in bitter circumstances.

Artemisia absinthium
COMMON WORMWOOD, MUGWORT

An attractive herbaceous perennial growing to about 90–150cm (3–5ft) in height, with deeply cut silvery grey foliage and spikes of little yellow-green flowers. It will grow in poor soil. Wormwood is largely the basis of 'bitters' and vermouths and other aperitif drinks as well as being essential in the make-up of absinthe and Pernod-like drinks. It is used but seldom in the kitchen or home today, but it was once a vital weapon against parasitic worms. Branches of plants were said to keep fleas and similar insects away if strewn on the floors.

CULTIVATION Plants can be grown from seed or cuttings. Seed should be sown in spring in shallow drills in full sun. Cuttings can be taken in summer and roots divided and planted at the same time. Wormwood makes a very useful border plant with its silver grey aromatic foliage. The variety 'Lambrook Silver' is recommended.

USES Wormwood foliage, dried and collected in sachets, can be used against moths and household insects. Infusions are said to be good against various stomach troubles and to clean the blood. They are probably highly unpleasant and it is suggested that those who wish to partake of the herb can best do so in the form of commercial drinks.

Below Southernwood, unsuitable for cooking, is a decorative shrub which tolerates city gardens. To promote foliage, the plant is cut back in spring to two buds of the previous year's growth

Above This aromatic, finely leaved herb, mugwort, grows wild, often on wasteland. The flower shoots are cut from mid to late summer, and the buds used as seasoning. Its properties are reputed to ease rheumatism

Below There are two varieties of tarragon, the French and the Russian (*Artemisia dracunculus*), but only the first is considered worth growing for use as flavouring in meat, fish and vegetable dishes, and for adding to sauces

Artemisia dracunculus
TARRAGON

Tarragon is a hardy, herbaceous, aromatic perennial growing to about 60–120cm (2–4ft), with entire, slender, dark green, pointed leaves and little clusters of greyish flowers that fail to open in most summers in this country. Two varieties, French and Russian, are grown, the former being the more popular.

CULTIVATION Grows best in a warm and protected site. Cut plants right back in autumn and in cold districts cover the rootstock with a protective coating of straw. Ordinary soil will do but full sun is essential. Allow plenty of space for the spreading roots. To propagate divide the roots in March or April by pulling apart the underground runners. Feed occasionally during the growing season but do not allow plants to become too lush. Every two or three years it is advisable to divide and replant to obtain strong growth. Plants can be lifted and grown in a frame or indoors in a light soil and given as much light as possible.

USES Tarragon is one of the most widely used herbs in cookery, both in its fresh and dried forms. It is essential to some classic sauces such as tartare and Béarnaise. It is an ingredient of fines herbes, mayonnaise, many pickles and preserves. It is frequently used in conjunction with chervil. Vinegar can be tarragon flavoured.

Artemisia vulgaris
MUGWORT

A herbaceous perennial with a woody rootstock growing to about 60–120cm (2–4ft) tall, with long, slender, divided leaves, dark green above and with a silvery white down on the undersides. The stems are a purple-red colour. The tiny dull yellow flowers in slim panicles appear in late summer.

CULTIVATION Increase by root or stem cuttings in spring. Plants are tolerant of soil and sun and grow easily.

USES Mugwort is a plant growing widely in the wild in many countries. It was once used for flavouring beer and the flowering stem tips were used in the preparation of a special stuffing for fatty poultry such as geese. Foliage and roots can be dried and used as a flavouring, but as a whole mugwort has been superceded by the more powerful and better flavoured tarragon.

Asperula odorata
WOODRUFF

A carpeting, groundcover, fragrant, native perennial about 30cm (12in) tall with whorls of slightly glossy green leaves and small, white, starry flowers. It grows wild in woods and uncultivated, shaded areas, flowering in late spring. When dried it smells of newly cut grass or new-mown hay.

CULTIVATION Seeds should be sown in summer as soon as they are ripe, choosing a site in light shade and a moist soil. As seeds sometimes take a long time to germinate it is usually quicker to divide the roots of established plants and place portions in the soil in light shade about 60cm (2ft) apart. After continuous cultivation for a period, self-sown plants will appear and cover the area.

USES Woodruff leaves give something special to a fruit punch made with white wine and/or champagne and plenty of succulent seasonal fruits. A refreshing tisane can also be made with the leaves used alone. At one time the dried leaves were mixed with tea as an economy measure. Leaves can be dried and put into sachets or similar packs for placing with linen, both to keep away moths and to spread their delightful scent.

Left Borage's vivid blue star-shaped flowers are not only highly attractive but edible too. According to the Elizabethan herbalist John Gerard, they lead to exhilaration and have the capacity to drive away the sorrows

Borago officinalis
BORAGE

A strong, upright annual growing to about 60cm (2ft) in almost any soil, preferably in sun. It is noted in particular for its flowers, which are favourites of bees, a characteristic deep bright blue, five-petalled, each bearing a central cone of black anthers. Buds and stems are covered with soft, greyish or silvery hairs that shine in the sun and help make the plant such an attractive one. Leaves are large, grey-green, also hairy.

CULTIVATION Borage is grown from seed sown in spring or late summer in good soil in a sunny site. The plant seeds freely and, under normal circumstances, once it is grown in the garden seedlings will be found in various places for ever after. It grows quickly and is mature in less than two months. If local soil is too heavy or damp for self-seeding, seeds may be sown in a seedbox in pots in early spring and the young plants placed in the garden soil a few weeks later.

USES Borage flowers look so attractive floating in a wine cup that their use as decoration seems to have taken precedence over any other. Flowers and leaves can be eaten, although the hairs on the foliage become stiff and unappetising as the plant ages and only the young leaves should be picked. If foliage is finely chopped the leaf hairs do not obtrude and the resulting greenery, slightly cucumber-flavoured, can be used as a dressing in salads.

Flowers can also be candied, or both flowers and leaves can be dipped in a light batter and deep fried as an unusual vegetable. The very slight cucumber flavour is lost if an attempt is made to dry and preserve either flowers or foliage.

Below For use as an air freshener woodruff is best cut in spring just before flowering. Drying the leaves develops the perfume which is useful for removing musty smells and moths from cupboards

Above The taste of pot marigold, a plant thought to have originated in India, is distinct from saffron, but simmering the petals will produce a similarly orange-coloured liquid which may be used to flavour dishes

Right With mint-scented leaves that have the flavour of lemon, alecost is harvested both for tisanes and for potpourri. The plant is propagated by root division as it will not seed in temperate climates

Calendula officinalis
POT MARIGOLD

The familiar orange-flowered marigold, grown as a decorative plant in our flower borders for centuries, has been known for just as long for its qualities as a dye, as a food and as a medicine. It is an annual, low growing, with oval green leaves and medium to large flowers with rays of yellow through orange to almost red. If flowers are systematically dead-headed, the plants will continue to replace them until the frosts.

CULTIVATION Marigolds like the sun but will grow almost anywhere. Like most hardy annuals they are normally grown from seed sown in autumn or spring. They are so easy that if plants are left to go to seed they will self-seed in the immediate neighbourhood.

USES Marigold flower petals give both flavour and colour when added to rice dishes, salads, cakes and puddings. They can be used as a substitute for saffron. The leaves are slightly bitter, even salty, and can be added to salads, but the petals are more often used for this purpose. Flower petals can also be dried. They can be used to make a tea, or blended with oils to produce an ointment which is said to clear the skin from old wounds and scratches. They are used as a rinse to condition and lighten blonde hair.

Carum carvi
CARAWAY

Caraway is a dainty herbaceous biennial which grows to about 60cm (2ft), with a feathery, carrot-like foliage and umbels of small white flowers in early summer. When ripe the fruits split into two crescent-shaped seeds, dark brown and full of flavour. It is one of the most ancient, and one of the most popular, of spices, still used today in great quantities.

CULTIVATION The plant grows well in ordinary well-drained soils. It will not tolerate winter wet. Seed should be sown in a prepared bed in spring or late summer in drills about 5cm (2in) deep, young plants later thinned to about 20cm (8in) apart and left undisturbed, except for weeding, until the following year. It grows easily and well and if seed is not collected it will self-seed, sometimes to an embarrassing extent. As soon as the seed ripens, usually in July or August, it should be collected. The seed stems should be hung, head downwards, in a cool, dry spot in small bunches, enclosed in a plastic bag or hung over sheets of newspaper so that the seed may be collected without waste. If plants die down in the winter they should be cut back severely so that they will grow again in the spring.

USES Seeds are used mainly in bakery, for breads, cakes and biscuits. Leaves and softer stems can also be eaten, usually in salads, with soft cheeses or cooked with other vegetables. The

Left Caraway occurs widely in Europe, Scandinavia, Russia and North America, and is now grown commercially. In the garden sow seeds where you require them as the plant does not transplant easily

flavour is mild and something like parsley. Even the thick roots can be consumed and are said to be parsnip-like in flavour. Caraway seed can also be added to soups, stews and meat dishes. A few grains of seed alone are said to dispel odours such as might remain from eating garlic and can be used generally to sweeten the breath.

Chrysanthemum balsamita
ALECOST, BIBLELEAF, COSTMARY, ALLSPICE, MACE

An herbaceous perennial with long, slim, green leaves with a hint of grey and a creeping rootstock, growing to a height of about 60–90cm (2–3ft). The small flowers, which open only in bright sun, have white petals and bright yellow centres. The name 'alecost' developed from the custom of adding a powdered costmary to ale to give it a slight astringency or bitterness, and the name 'bibleleaf' came from the habit of using a leaf in a bible as a bookmark. The trivial name 'mace' indicates that the flavour of the leaves is similar to the spice.

CULTIVATION Alecost is propagated by division of the roots in autumn or spring. Plant the divisions in light, rich soil in full sun.

USES Because of its soft, minty aroma, alecost is used chopped in salads or a single leaf is used to flavour soups and sauces. Taste and perfume are strong and some care should be exercised because they may be too powerful for the dish. Partly because of the power of the perfume, alecost is popular for use as a potpourri ingredient, where the aroma spreads through the other materials to intensify them all.

In medieval times when use of the herb was at a peak, it was employed powdered for stomach upsets and made into an ointment to soothe burns, bruises and other skin blemishes or wounds. It was also rubbed into bee stings.

Cochlearia armoracia
HORSERADISH

A hardy perennial with long, elliptical, dark green leaves somewhat reminiscent of dock. It grows to a height of about 60cm (2ft) with erect stems on which, in good summers, appear small, scented, four-petalled white flowers producing round seed pods which seldom ripen in this country. The plant is believed to have come from eastern Europe and to have been known and used for thousands of years. It is grown for its thick, fleshy, aromatic roots, hot, pungent and full of flavour, used mainly with strong meats as an antidote to their richness and as the basis of a sauce or a dressing. It has the alternative botanical name of *Armoracia rusticana*.

CULTIVATION Horseradish grows in ordinary deep soil. It is propagated easily from root cuttings. In winter cut pencil-thick portions of about 15cm (6in) long from side roots. Plant these right side up 10cm (4in) below the soil surface and about 20cm (8in) apart. As a rule no great quantity of horseradish will be needed, so no large area need be devoted to it as a crop and, because it is invasive and difficult to eradicate completely when growing strongly, it is sometimes wise to grow horseradish in a distant and even neglected part of the garden. However, the soil must be rich enough to result in plump roots rather than mere strings.

USES Horseradish sauce uses grated roots mixed with cream or some similar viscous liquid. It must be used raw, for cooked roots lose their flavour. Roots can be grated and dried and stored in airtight containers for later use. The leaves also are pungent and tasty and can be chopped and used as a salad ingredient. Leaves were once used externally as a dressing to salve burns and skin wounds.

Below Known in central Europe since the Middle Ages, the fleshy white roots of the vigorous horseradish are used in a cream sauce as a condiment with roast beef. The plant is also said to have antibiotic properties

Above Though they tolerate freezing, the leaves of coriander do not dry well. The spicy seeds, the main harvest, are added to liqueurs and pickles, besides a wide range of sweet and savoury dishes

Below Similar to dill in appearance, with which it may cross pollinate, fennel grows wild in Britain often in chalky soil and along the coasts

Coriandrum sativum
CORIANDER

An attractive hardy annual growing to about 60cm (2ft) with slim green stems bearing divided green leaves, heavier near the base than at the top. The small, pinkish flowers appear in summer, followed by the round fruits.

When these fruits or seeds are ripe the plant should be cut down and dried over newspapers to collect the seeds as they fall.

CULTIVATION Sow the seed in 1cm (½in) deep drills in spring in a light, rich soil in full sun. The seeds will gradually change from green to a brownish grey in late summer and it is most helpful to cut down the plants just before they are fully ripe rather than wait until they are fully mature, for in this case some of the seed is sure to be dropped and lost.

USES Fresh green coriander leaves, known as cilantro or Chinese parsley, are much used in Eastern cookery. Stalks also are highly regarded and used especially with beans and soups for flavouring. Roots are used in some countries to flavour curry pastes.

Coriander seed is generally used ground. It is blended with curry and spice mixtures and gives an extra flavour to stuffings and dressings for poultry and game. It is used both whole and ground in bread and cake baking. Less obvious is its background use to flavour and render more palatable certain medicines, sweets and liqueurs. An old-fashioned sweet was sugar-coated coriander seeds.

Foeniculum vulgare
FENNEL

A hardy perennial which will grow up to 2m (6ft) tall, with leaves so finely cut as to be almost hair-like. The large, stiff umbels of small yellow flowers are followed by the anise-aromatic seeds. There is a beautiful bronze-leaved variety. Stems, leaves and seeds have their culinary uses. Leaves need to be young to provide greatest perfume and flavour. Fennel will seed itself and, although native, it often escapes from gardens to grow wild.

Grown for its bulbous stem bases, the variety Florence fennel, or finocchio, is largely eaten raw in salads, having again the characteristic anise flavour and smell. Its leaves and seeds can be used in the same way as those of the common fennel.

CULTIVATION Fennel grows best in a rich, well-drained soil in full sun. Seeds can be sown in autumn or spring and plants can be divided in spring. Foliage can be cut for use from early spring until autumn, but before winter sets in it is as well to cut down the plants to some 10cm (4in) from the ground.

Finocchio needs a deep, moist soil and the plants should be earthed up slightly as they grow in order to obtain good, fat stem bases. Water during dry periods and cut down any flower stems as soon as they appear.

USES Fennel is used mainly as a flavouring for fish or some of the blander meats such as pork and veal. It can be added to soups, sauces and to prepared cheeses. Stems, first peeled, can be added to salads. Seeds are widely used in Indian cookery and by bakers for breads and cakes. Seeds can be roasted. Dried stalks are used for grilled fish. Finocchio, raw, grated or sliced, goes well in salads or by itself with cheese. Stewed, it accompanies veal.

Humulus lupulus
HOPS

An attractive, twining, perennial climber, grown commercially for its fruits which are used in the preparation of beers, and found also in the wild, growing in hedges or among trees. It and its golden form, 'Aureus', are cultivated for their decorative value in gardens. The leaves are large and pale green; the male flowers small, greenish yellow, carried in loose bunches and the actual 'hops', the female flowers, in cone-like catkins. The little powdery fruits contained in the female flowers are the source of the lupulin, a somewhat bitter substance which helps to flavour beers.

CULTIVATION By seeds sown in ordinary soil in spring, or by the division of roots at roughly the same time. The soil should be rich, deep and in full sun to give the best plants and the protection of a wall or fence on which the climber can twine will also help. Roots should never be allowed to dry out and plenty of water should be applied in times of drought. The female flowers should be gathered in September if it is wished to use them, and the whole plant should be cut down almost to ground level in October. The plants grow so quickly that they can be used to make a pleasant, leafy screen in summer. *H.l.* 'Aureus', the golden form, does not fruit so generously as the species.

USES Female hop flowers or fruits are used in the manufacture of beers. Young hop shoots are said to make a good boiled vegetable, but medicinally they can be so powerful that it might be unwise to eat too lavishly. Pillows filled with dried hop flowers are said to induce sleep.

Hyssopus officinalis
HYSSOP

A low-growing, aromatic, semi-evergreen shrub which reaches some 60cm (2ft) and produces single-sided spikes of flowers which are normally a rich blue but can be pink or white. The foliage is dark green, slim, entire. The plant appears to have come originally from the Middle East, via southern Europe and is now established even in more northern parts and in the United States.

CULTIVATION This fairly hardy shrub makes little demand and will tolerate ordinary soil and sun or light shade. Seeds should be sown in early spring and seedlings planted out to about 60cm (2ft) apart in June and July. Alternatively, hyssop can be grown from cuttings taken in April and May and by the division of roots, either in spring or autumn. Keep well watered when young.

USES The pungent aroma and the strong, slightly bitter taste of hyssop make it a herb to be treated with some delicacy in cooking. It is used to counteract excessive fat in some meats and fish dishes and it is sometimes added, finely chopped, to salads or used as a garnish in soups and stews. Hyssop is an ingredient in several liqueurs and has been made into a tea said to be good for bronchial complaints. Bees are attracted by the flowers.

Above Hops are normally used in beer making and they are also used to fill sleep pillows

Below Hyssop, an ingredient of Chartreuse liqueur, is an attractive blue-flowered shrub that can be cultivated as a hedge

Inula helenium
ELECAMPANE

A vigorous hardy herbaceous perennial which will grow as tall as 2m (6ft) and sometimes more, with large green leaves and clusters of large, somewhat coarse, but very distinctive daisy-like yellow flowers produced in mid-summer. The leaves are a deep green above, lighter below, with a downy, hairy surface. The plant grows wild in many parts of the world, mainly where the soil is moist and open to the sun.

CULTIVATION Seeds can be sown in spring or the plants can be divided, preferably also in spring as autumn propagation can be made difficult by cold weather. Almost instant propagation is provided by taking offsets, each with a good portion of root and a strong bud. Spring is the best time.

USES The roots of elecampane were once used in cooking as a flavouring. They were also eaten salted and candied. The roots are bitter tasting, pungent and warming and were recommended for bronchial complaints. Roots were made into confectionary and given to children with coughs and sneezes. Steeped in some wines it was said to ward off indigestion after a meal and to have other influences, as Gerard states that wine prepared with the root of elecampane 'wonderfully quickens the sight'.

Isatis tinctoria
WOAD

An herbaceous biennial growing to 1m (3ft) or more in height, producing long, broad, greyish green leaves up its stems in the first year and plentiful panicles of small, four-petalled, honey-scented yellow flowers in the summer of the following year. These flowers are followed by the fruits, green at first, then turning brown and finally blue-black when they are ripe.

CULTIVATION Sow the seeds outdoors on rich, moist soil in a sunny situation in the late spring, or earlier in boxes in a greenhouse or frame. Plant out seedlings about 1m (3ft) apart. Plants grow well and easily and will self-sow.

USES Although mainly known as a dye, woad was used medicinally as an ointment against skin diseases and ulcers. Because it was believed to help in the cure of skin wounds, warriors sometimes painted themselves with woad before battle. As a dye, woad is prepared by collecting leaves in the first year, grinding or pulping them and allowing them to ferment. The resulting liquid is mixed with lime-water to produce the dye.

Juniperus communis
JUNIPER

An evergreen shrub with small, sharp, grey-green leaves like short, thick needles, found both wild and cultivated in many parts of the world. Stems can be almost prostrate on windy, shallow-soiled hillsides, but in a softer environment the plant grows to a 3m (10ft) tree. In summer it produces small cones at leaf and stem junctions, yellow on male plants and blue-green on female. Gradually the female cones become berry-like, changing from green to black over a period of some three years. It is these ripe 'berries' which are used to flavour gin and for medicinal and culinary purposes.

CULTIVATION Junipers will grow in almost any situation and in almost any soil, but are often found growing wild on calcareous soils. Propagation from seed takes a very long time as germination may not occur until after 12 months, so cuttings are usually taken, young shoots of the current year's growth being placed in sandy soil in a cold frame in autumn.

If juniper plants are being grown make sure that both sexes are included in your scheme so that a crop of the useful berries can be produced. Plant them in the same area but the plants need not actually touch.

Right Juniper berries picked in autumn and popularly used to flavour gin, are also excellent in marinades for game, pork, mutton and poultry

USES The berries are time-consuming and tedious to pick, so when they are ripe it is easiest, where sufficient supplies exist and no significant damage will be done to trees, to collect whole branches here and there to be stripped of berries in the comfort of home. The berries must be dried before use and they are not damaged when dried in sun.

Leaves are occasionally used with discretion, but it is generally the berries which are used in cooking, sometimes whole, but more frequently crushed with a pestle and mortar. Strong meats and game, chicken liver and kidney dishes are improved by the aroma and flavour of the crushed berries and, with care, other meats, generally roasted, can also be so flavoured.

Laurus nobilis
BAY

The true laurel is an aromatic, evergreen tree, hardy is most districts, often grown clipped and trained in a tub or other container, but reaching 10m (33ft) or so sometimes in its native Mediterranean locale. The leaves are small, shining, dark green on top and a softer, greenish yellow on the underside, almost downy. In early summer small greenish yellow flowers appear in the axils of the leaves, to be followed by purple berries.

CULTIVATION Seed is both difficult to obtain and to germinate. Young plants are grown either from cuttings, 8–10cm (3–4in) long, inserted in sandy soil in late summer under a cloche or in a propagating case — for bottom heat is helpful — or by layering stems in autumn when this is possible. Young plants should go out into a prepared and sheltered bed in good soil, well drained and warm.

Alternatively, grow in a pot, gradually training the young specimen into the shape you desire. To do this, cut the leaves individually from their stems rather than clipping the whole of the growth with shears, for this will result in cut and wounded leaves, which are unpleasant and unslightly. Save clippings to dry and use. It is wise to give bay trees protection against extreme cold and strong winds, so in winter either bring tubs indoors or protect plants by a wall or other wind shield.

USES Laurel wreaths, with which victors at cultural festivals are crowned, are usually made of plastic these days, so bay reverts entirely to its culinary purposes. A bay leaf is an essential ingredient of a bouquet garni and individual leaves, sometimes half-leaves, are used in soups, stews, meat and some vegetable dishes and in milk puddings. In old recipes the term 'laurel leaf' is used for bay.

Leaves can be somewhat bitter when fresh, so dried leaves are frequently used as the flavour appears to soften and the aroma to increase in this process. Dry them in the dark and under cool, dry conditions. Leaves are reputed to protect against insects and for this purpose are added to stores of flour, pulses and similar foods. They are also an ingredient of potpourris and similar products.

Lavandula
LAVENDER

There are many different species, varieties and forms of lavender, differing in the size of the plants or the flower spikes, the colour of the flowers and the strength of the perfume. None of these differences need concern us here, all types being basically hardy, bushy shrubs with small, slim, grey-green leaves and flowers which vary from the somewhat rare white through tints and shades of 'lavender' or mauve and pink to a comparatively bright purple. Scent is strongest in the flowers, which are the source of the aromatic oils, but all parts of the plant are perfumed to some degree. Plants grow wild in many parts of the world, but Mediterranean regions are accepted as the lavender's most comfortable home.

CULTIVATION Lavender enjoys the sun and an open position with rich, but well-drained, soil on the limy side of the pH scale will suit it best. It is possible to grow plants from seed and self-sown plants occur, but cuttings are generally

Below A favourite in the bath with the Romans and Greeks, lavender today is normally placed in sachets for its perfume. More unusually the flowers may be crystallized for cake decoration

used for propagation. Take young green shoots, about 5–10cm (2–4in) long, in spring or in autumn, remove the lower leaves and insert the stems in a sandy compost in boxes or pots in a frame, or with some similar protection. Cuttings taken in spring will root in a few weeks but those taken later in the year will be slower.

Keep plants well trimmed to prevent them becoming too woody and straggling. As the flower buds open collect them with long stems and allow the flowers to dry spread out well on newspaper. Keep the stems to use as scented firelighters.

USES Lavender was once perhaps the best of the strewing herbs to place on the floor to sweeten the atmosphere of a foetid room. The same effect to a lesser degree is achieved by the more modern method of making up the flowers into sachets and distributing these in drawers among linen or clothes. Much lavender is used in the preparation of toilet waters and perfumes and today only small quantities have culinary uses, mainly in conserves. It is also grown in considerable quantities in private gardens, as bushes or as hedges to divide one part of the garden from another. Here regular trimming is necessary to keep plants under control.

Levisticum officinale
LOVAGE

A tall, hardy, perennial plant growing to 2m (6ft) or so in good, rich, moist soil. It produces dark green, shiny leaves growing from the hollow stems. In midsummer umbels of yellow flowers appear, to be followed by curved, brown, oval fruits. The seed, usually crushed, is used in the preparation of some Mediterranean dishes. Plants die down to the ground in winter and in spring shoot upwards again, this time a beautiful, glistening bronze colour while very young.

CULTIVATION Lovage can be grown from seed, sown as soon as it is ripe, but more frequently propagation is carried out by dividing the fleshy roots so that each piece bears a strong bud. The situation can be in sun or light shade. Ordinary soil will suit, but if the soil is deep, enriched and moist, the plants will grow more freely.

USES The strong celery flavour of lovage is useful when brought to soups, stews and casseroles and it is frequently added, fresh or dried, to certain vegetarian dishes. The leaves maintain their flavour when boiled for long periods. A handful of leaves, used raw, is sometimes rubbed into meat before roasting. Fresh leaves are also added to salads and vegetables. Seeds give flavour and texture to breads and savoury and cheese dishes. Roots can be used in cooking, but are frequently found to be too strongly flavoured unless carefully peeled.

Marrubium vulgare
HOREHOUND

A hardy perennial plant with wrinkled, greenish white leaves covered with hairs, equally hairy stems and tiny white flowers, which grows to about 60cm (2ft) and enjoys heat, sun and drought. Horehound is a member of *Labiatae*, the mint family.

CULTIVATION Horehound grows strongly and easily from seed sown on poor and arid soil, but it will have a longer life if the soil is enriched with moist compost or well-rotted farmyard manure. Cuttings are also easy to root. Leaves should be harvested and dried when the flowers appear.

USES Once used for flavouring beer, as a cough cure and expectorant, a healer of ulcers, as a febrifuge and in veterinary practice for horse ailments. Nowadays it has found its way into the decorative flower borders, where its silvery grey appearance makes it useful in certain colour schemes.

Left All parts of lovage, a vigorous plant which takes about four years to reach full size, can be used for herbal purposes. Chopped leaves may be added to casseroles and infused for tisanes

Above The golden variegated variety of lemon balm makes this an attractive garden shrub. The plant, heavily scented, is also invaluable for drawing bees, and according to Culpepper, for driving away 'all troublesome cares'

Right Mints have been harvested for culinary use probably since neolithic times in southern Europe. This hybrid peppermint is a cross between water mint and spearmint, and itself has two forms, black peppermint and white peppermint

Melilotus officinalis
MELILOT

A member of the pea family, *Leguminosae*, once grown as a fodder crop and to flavour beers, melilot has become wild, growing on roadsides and railway embankments. It grows to some 60–90cm (2–3ft), has trifoliate green leaves and attractive, characteristically pea-like, yellow flowers, white in one variety. Both the perfume and the flavour of melilot resemble hay, the scent being enhanced when the herb is dried.

CULTIVATION The plant grows wild. Otherwise sow seed in autumn or spring in any soil in a sunny situation.

USES Melilot is beloved by bee keepers, for it is in flower over a long period, produces nectar in great quantities and is attractive to bees, probably because of the scent.

Melissa officinalis
LEMON BALM

A perennial growing to about 1m (3ft), lemon balm or simply balm, has leaves similar to those of the nettle and small, white, somewhat insignificant flowers. It has become wild in many parts and grows

prolifically when established. This also is a good plant for bees, but those without hives may prefer to cut off all flowers as they appear in order to obtain a better crop of the lemon-scented, lemon-flavoured leaves.

CULTIVATION Lemon balm can be grown from seed, from root division and from cuttings. Sow seeds in spring or autumn on rich, moist soil in a warm, protected, sunny position. Roots can be divided, also in autumn or spring. Cuttings are best taken in summer. It grows early in the spring and spreads rapidly.

The leaves can be picked as they are required, or if so wished, the whole of the foliage can be cut in spring, which will encourage another crop to appear by the summer. Earlier crops have the largest and most flavoursome leaves. If the leaves are to be dried, use the first shoots, ready when the flowers begin to open. Dry them quickly but take care not to bruise them.

USES Chopped fresh leaves are used with poultry and fish dishes and sauces and in salads. They provide a delicate lemon tang for jams and jellies. A leaf or two gives zest to a cool summer fruit cup and both fresh and dried leaves make perhaps some of the best and most enjoyable herbal teas. Lemon balm is sometimes planted in fruit orchards to attract bees which will pollinate the fruit blossom.

Mentha
MINT

There are many mints, wild and cultivated, many natural hybrids, many different mints with identical names, many with differences so slight that only microscopic examination can separate them. In view of these facts, the best-known mints are described here under the names that are substantiated by the authority of the Royal Horticultural Society and as the differences are minor and their cultivation and uses very much the same, I propose only to mention them briefly here and to separate their uses where there are any.

Spearmint, *Mentha spicata*, is probably the best known of the culinary mints and one which does not occur in the wild except as a garden escape. It grows to about 30–40cm (12–16in), is hairless, with lanceolate, bright green leaves and lilac flowers.

Apple mint, *M. rotundifolia*, known also as *M. suaveolens*, is frequently grown in its variegated form with its rounder leaves splashed with cream and magenta. It is sometimes called pineapple mint.

Peppermint, *M. piperita*, is very likely a cross between the original mint, *M. aquatica* and the spearmint, *M. spicata*.

All the mints are perennial, have four-sided stems with parallel, opposite leaves on short stalks, spikes of small white, pink or purple flowers in summer. They all grow from invasive underground runners which are normally prevented from travelling too far by growing the plant in a bottomless bucket or by enclosing the roots within walls of slate or stone. All are distinguished by the strong and characteristic perfume of the oils, so important in cooking and in the flavouring and perfuming of many products from toothpastes and chewing gum to liqueurs and perfumes.

CULTIVATION Grow the mints from pieces of root about 15cm (6in) long, taken in spring and placed some 5cm (2in) deep in a well-cultivated, moist soil in light shade. Make sure the roots are controlled and prevented from travelling too far. A few roots can be potted up and grown indoors for kitchen use during the winter. The leaves can be dried.

USES Although spearmint is best known and most widely grown, apple mint, round-leaved and hairy, is best for the usual culinary purposes such as the preparation of mint sauce and addition to boiled peas, potatoes and the like. The leaf hairs are not important and are not noticed when leaves are chopped or boiled. Mint leaves are added to salads, salad dressings and many meat and vegetable dishes.

Monarda didyma
BERGAMOT

A North American herbaceous perennial which grows to about 1m (3ft) with red flowers and perfumed, slightly toothed, hairy leaves. The red bergamot is known also as bee balm, because of its attraction for bees, and as Oswego tea, it being said that the Oswego tribe of American Indians enjoyed a drink brewed from the leaves. Today bergamot is largely a decorative garden plant and several varieties with different colours are cultivated for garden use.

CULTIVATION Bergamot is propagated by division of the fibrous, almost woody roots in autumn or spring. Plants can sometimes be difficult to establish

Below The mop heads of bergamot, which may be white, pink, mauve, or scarlet, are eye-catching above the plant's abundant foliage. The lemon-scented leaves are a good addition to salads and pork dishes

where the soil is dry or cold, but a rich, warm, moist soil will ensure strong and healthy clumps of plants which grow so rapidly that they have to be divided every two or three years. Make sure that the roots are kept moist. In warm gardens light shade might be a better location for the plants than full sun.

USES Bergamots are favourite border plants. Some are grown only for use in potpourri. However, they can be used in cooking. Those who find the taste of sage too strong may care to try bergamot leaves instead with roast pork. Entire florets can be used as a garnish for a salad as well as chopped leaves. Oil of bergamot comes from a citrus fruit, not from this plant.

Myrrhis odorata
SWEET CICELY

An attractive, tall-growing, perennial herb which lasts almost the whole year through and is decorative all of this time. It has pretty, finely divided leaves and characteristic umbels of white flowers in early summer. The flowers, which smell of anise, develop into fruits or seeds, dark brown and shining, which can be up to 2cm (¾in) long. The plant grows so well and easily that it can be found wild in Britain and many parts of Europe.

CULTIVATION Light shade and a moist, deep soil will help sweet cicely to

Above and below If given a damp, shady spot, sweet cicely will be the first herb to arrive in spring and the last to die down in autumn. It will also seed itself readily in the garden

grow well and seed itself. Otherwise fresh seed can be sown in spring or autumn or roots can be divided in summer. As plants will grow to more than 1m (3ft) they should not be planted too closely or they will be overcrowded. The new leaves appear early in the spring, followed by flowers in early summer. The green seeds can be gathered and used as soon as they have grown to a useful size. Flowers continue to appear throughout summer.

USES It is particularly useful, because all parts of the plant can be eaten and all parts are sweet, so that it can help replace sugar or reduce amounts needed in certain dishes, to the benefit of any one on a diabetic diet. The fruits can be chopped when green and used in salads and, when brown and ripe, can be added whole to pies and similar dishes.

Myrtus communis
MYRTLE

A tall, sweet-smelling, evergreen shrub, which when grown in a tub, as is usual in our gardens, is unlikely to become more than 60–90cm (2–3ft) tall, but in its native Mediterranean soil can reach 5m (16½ft). The leaves are glossy, green and aromatic, the flowers are soft creamy white, growing singly or in clusters and the fruits are blue-black. Plants in pots can be clipped and trained to shape.

CULTIVATION If myrtle is to be grown in open soil, choose a sheltered site away from strong winds where the soil is moist, rich and deep. Protect from frosts during winter. Propagate by layering. Make sure the roots of young plants are never allowed to become too dry.

USES Both leaves and berries are used to flavour and also as a stuffing for game and strong meats. Branches are sometimes burned or kept smouldering to smoke roast meats and impart a special aromatic flavour to them. Leaves and flowers are dried and used in potpourris and for perfumery.

Ocimum basilicum
BASIL

Basil is grown as a perennial in its native India, but by the time it has travelled halfway round the world to Britain it

must be treated as an annual. In India it is a holy herb among the Hindus; in Greece its base name 'Basileus' indicates that it is a king among herbs, and in several Mediterranean countries pots of basil are presented as gifts between friends. It is esteemed both as a culinary gift and as a means of keeping away flies. It grows to about 50–100cm (20–40in) and has wide, perfumed, fleshy leaves and spikes of purplish white flowers.

There are several varieties, the sweet basil, *O. basilicum* being the best, although a number of modern hybrids cannot be ignored. It was one of the old strewing herbs and is still used as a fly deterrent. It is widely used in the kitchen in many savoury dishes.

CULTIVATION Basil should be grown from seed sown under glass and planted out in a warm and sheltered spot no earlier than June. Soil should be rich, light, well drained and kept constantly moist. Flower buds should be pinched out as they develop in order to obtain strong and bushy growth. Stems or leaves can be kept for a short period in a refrigerator in a sealed plastic bag, or rather longer in the deep freeze after being quickly blanched. Dried leaves seem to change their flavour and taste almost like one of the curries.

USES Basil is widely used in the kitchen but the leaves should be added at the end of the cooking process rather than allowing them to stew, bake or boil. It is an important ingredient in the making of the well-known pesto sauce (see page 72). It has the capacity of enhancing the flavour of tomatoes and goes well with many other herbs and with mushroom dishes.

Origanum
MARJORAM

Of the several marjorams grown in this country, three stand out as important in the herbal and culinary field. *Origanum majorana* is the sweet marjoram, a half-hardy annual here, making a small bush up to about 30cm (12in) tall, with greyish, hairy leaves and pale pink or white flowers. Sweet or knotted marjoram is comparatively mild, safe to use in quantity but not the favourite of the gastronome or the experienced cook. *Origanum onites*, pot marjoram, is a little larger, growing to some 60cm (2ft),

with hairy stems and small leaves and again with pink or white flowers.

CULTIVATION Sweet marjoram can be grown from seed sown in March in a frame or greenhouse or on a sunny windowsill, plants being transferred to the open ground in late May or early June when all fear of frosts is past. It is often very slow to germinate.

Pot and wild marjorams are easier to propagate because they are less dependent on warmth. Seed can be sown in spring, the roots may be divided in spring or autumn or cuttings can be taken early in summer. Full sun and a certain amount of protection help to ensure good crops.

USES The marjorams are among the most important of the culinary herbs and, as might be expected, they are essential

Below Marjoram, a herb popular for highly flavoured meat and vegetable dishes, is an attractive feature in the garden when in flower

to many dishes which originate in Mediterranean areas, pizzas, pastas, grilled goat and lamb dishes. They go well with cheeses and tomato. Unless you have a taste for robust Italian, Sicilian or Greek peasant dishes, you might be wise to use sweet marjoram rather than the wild, or to temper the quantities used according to your palate.

Papaver somniferum
OPIUM POPPY

An attractive flowering annual about 1m (3ft) tall, bearing on stems of striking glaucous grey-green, beautiful, large, pink to mauve, sometimes white, flowers in summer. When the petals fall the characteristic round, crowned seed vessel is left, green and sappy at first, ripening to light brown and bearing a multitude of seeds which in time are scattered on the ground to produce many self-sown plants. There are many beautiful double-flowered garden varieties such as paeony-flowered and carnation-flowered.

Below A native to Greece and the Far East the opium poppy produces seeds that may be used to decorate bread and cakes. A popular garden variety is 'Paeony-flowered Mixed'

CULTIVATION Sow seed in almost any soil or situation.

USES The green seed vessel is tapped to produce a milky fluid, the source of opium, from which is derived morphine and other drugs. The ripe seeds in the brown capsule are much used, being non-narcotic, in recipes of many countries, mostly as a flavouring and dressing for many cakes and breads.

Petroselinum crispum
PARSLEY

An herbaceous biennial with soft green foliage crisply curled. It is an important source of vitamins and minerals and has been one of the most popular of all herbs for everyday consumption for thousands of years. There is also a French parsley, with broader, uncurled foliage, and a form grown for its roots, the Hamburg parsley, also with uncurled leaves. Stems, sometimes called 'heads', cut for consumption are soon replaced and a steady supply is produced.

CULTIVATION If parsley is to be grown in succession, sow seeds from spring through to late summer. The seed must be fresh and the soil rich and moist. Where there is space allow some plants to flower and self-seed. Germination can take as long as eight weeks, but some gardeners maintain that this period can be halved if the seed is soaked in warm water before sowing, and if the drills in which it is sown have boiling water poured into them shortly before sowing. Seedlings should be thinned or transplanted to about 60cm (2ft). In dry summers transplanting can lead to bolting.

Plants can be protected by cloches or a frame in winter and can also be lifted or sown and grown indoors in pots. Hamburg parsley, which is a little parsnip-like, requires rather more space and a deeper soil to produce its fleshy roots. Leave these in the soil until they are required. The leaves also can be picked and used.

USES Parsley is an important ingredient of a bouquet garni. It is popularly used mainly as a garnish or for making parsley sauce, but it can play more important roles than this (see chapter six). It is a very rich source of minerals and vitamins.

Pimpinella anisum
ANISE

A tender annual requiring care and some coddling to grow well in this country, succeeding best in rare, hot summers. It grows only to about 20cm (8in), has broad and jagged lower leaves and finely divided and feathery upper leaves. Small white flowers are produced in umbels in late summer and, if the weather is warm, these are followed by brown seeds. Although it is difficult to grow this plant satisfactorily in this country, its flavour, that of anise, is basic to the culinary art and several other herbs of the same family, *Umbelliferae*, reflect it to lesser degrees.

CULTIVATION Propagation is by seed sown in late spring in a warm, sunny situation on a rich, but light and dry soil. Sow carefully as young plants do not transplant well. Keep young plants well weeded. Seeds take some time to germinate and require higher temperatures than we normally enjoy. If seeds appear and mature, collect the seed heads as they begin to colour and let them dry slowly.

USES Leaves can be eaten in salads, with vegetables and mild cheeses. The seeds can be used in cakes and breads but are more frequently employed in flavouring drinks such as Pernod and other strong alcoholic liquors.

Portulaca oleracea
PURSLANE

A low-growing (30cm/12in) hardy annual with thick, fleshy, oval green leaves and small yellow flowers in summer. It is said to be rich in vitamins, minerals and trace elements, which may explain why it has been eaten for centuries, mainly in India and the Middle East.

CULTIVATION Propagation is by seed, division of the roots, or by cuttings, all from about mid-April through until mid-summer. Choose light, rich soil in a sunny, warm, well-drained spot.

USES Young leaves can be added to summer salads and the stems cooked as a green vegetable. Purslane tea is said to be useful for blood disorders.

Rosmarinus officinalis
ROSEMARY

A leafy evergreen shrub which grows up to 2m (6ft) tall, with long, slim, almost straight-edged leaves, green above and whitish beneath. The small, light blue flowers, which appear in clusters in early summer, are attractive to bees. The leaves, looking almost as though they come from a conifer, are thickish and firm rather than succulent and they are the main source of the highly aromatic, almost spicy scent of the plant. Rosemary came originally from some of the more arid and scrub-like slopes in Mediterranean areas and it enjoys warm, dry conditions, so much so that it may need shelter or protection in some parts.

Left Parsley is rich in vitamins A and C and contains iodine and several minerals including iron. If you have not sown a succession of plants, cut the parsley down in September to encourage it to start new growth

Below Rosemary can be propagated from seed but it is more commonly grown from rooted cuttings taken from mid summer to early autumn. It grows best if planted near a wall

CULTIVATION Although it is a good shrub grown under favourable conditions, rosemary will last for up to ten years or so in a garden and unless it is cut it will become more and more straggling and woody. The more rosemary is used by the cook, the stockier will be the plant, otherwise cutting back growth each year after flowering will help. It is always a good plan to propagate new plants every three or four years. Take half-ripe cuttings and insert them in a sandy soil in the open during the summer. Good plants will be formed by the second year. The bushes can be attractive and decorative in the garden, either as specimens or to make a low hedge. There are several varieties, with either paler or brighter blue flowers, and with a more prostrate or a more upright form of growth.

USES After hundreds of years of being used as one of the most important culinary herbs, rosemary went out of fashion in this country as it was considered too strong for the somewhat flabby and mild dishes of a few years ago. If used at all, rosemary was introduced to a dish for only a few moments and then taken out again before the flavour could become too strong. Some cooks still maintain that leaves or sprigs of rosemary should always be removed before a dish is served, yet tender shoots need be no more offensive than mint or parsley. It is best with strong dishes, roasts, stews and in sauces and stuffings. Rosemary is also used in the preparation of perfumes and shampoos.

Rumex acetosa
SORREL

A perennial herb which grows to about 1m (3ft) tall, with wide, arrow-shaped leaves very much like docks, to which it is related, and with tall stems clustered with little red flowers in summer. A native plant in this country, it grows wild in many parts of the world. There are several varieties and nomenclature is somewhat muddled.

CULTIVATION Grows in ordinary soil, but appreciates moisture. Sow seed in spring or divide plants in autumn. Place plants well apart, say 45cm (18in), in order to provide every opportunity for them to make strong and succulent growth. Remove the flower stems as they appear. Gather the leaves frequently to prevent the plant becoming unproductive.

USES Sorrel leaves can be used in salads and cooked like spinach. Leaves also make a seasoning for vegetables and stews. Sorrel soup is a favourite dish in some areas of France. Meat is said to become tender if wrapped in leaves of some of the stronger varieties.

Ruta graveolens
RUE

A hardy evergreen shrub growing to about 60cm (2ft), with heavy, grey-blue, much divided, highly aromatic leaves, and strong-flavoured umbels of small yellow flowers all through the summer.

CULTIVATION Rue can be grown from seed, by cuttings or by division of the roots. It will grow well in poor soils but needs full sunlight.

USES Once esteemed as a strewing herb, an insect repellent and as protection against disease (judges of the court still carry bunches of rue in some ceremonies as a reminder that it was carried in former times to ward off plague). It was also used considerably in cooking, but today rue is a useful herbaceous decorative plant and little more. Some people find it to be a skin irritant.

Below Rue, a native of the Balkan peninsula, will make a good ornamental shrub if straggly shoots are pruned in late spring. In small quantities the bitter leaves may be used in cooking, but are possibly better for decoration

Salvia
SAGE

A hardy, woody shrub growing to about 60cm (2ft), with oval, grey-green slightly hairy leaves. The broad-leaved variety of the common sage frequently fails to flower in this country. When it does so the flowers are a pale blue, lilac or purple. There are something like 700 species of salvia, the most important as a herb being *S. officinalis*, the common sage. *S.o.* 'Purpurea' is a form called the red sage and there are other forms with gold, cream, red, purple and green leaves or splashed with these colours. Like so many herbs, sage came from Mediterranean regions and there it grows best, but it is so important a culinary herb that it is grown in most temperate parts of the world.

CULTIVATION Propagation is by softwood cuttings taken in late spring and grown in a frame or with some similar protection. Alternatively, take woody cuttings with a heel and place in an open, well-drained soil in summer. Plants should be grown in full sun in a slightly limy soil, strong, deep and well drained. Unless frequently picked, plants tend to grow straggly after a few years, in which case they should be cut back each spring and renewed every four or five years. Some protection from cold and damp in winter is always helpful; a good straw mulch will be sufficient. Sage makes a good pot plant, but as appearance with this method of cultivation is important, subjects should be trimmed to shape as and when necessary.

USES Sage is a favourite herb with the British. It is also important where strong, eastern Mediterranean dishes are being prepared. It is generally too strong a herb for more delicate French food. It is used as a stuffing and as an addition to sausage, veal, cheeses, lamb, goat and mutton. A number of sage cheeses are made. It is also a medicinal herb, used as a digestive, a blood tonic, an antiseptic, a tooth cleaner and a hair tonic.

Sambucus nigra
ELDER

A familiar deciduous bush or tree growing everywhere in ordinary soil on farmland in this country, frequently in a farm hedge where it is kept clipped to some

2m (6.6ft), but also as a free-standing tree allowed to reach 10m (33ft) or so. The leaves are a soft green and the flowers appear in corymbs of creamy white in early summer, developing into clusters of berries so dark red or purple that they are almost black. As is to be expected, the tree responds well to cutting back and replaces lost growth quickly and vigorously. The whole tree gives off a vague, heavy and to some people slightly unpleasant odour. There are many attractive and highly decorative garden varieties.

CULTIVATION Most easily propagated by taking cuttings in autumn. If necessary prune into shape in winter.

USES Both flowers and berries are widely used for making home-made drinks such as elderflower champagne and elderberry wine. The flowers can be coated with a thin batter and deep fried. The berries are used in jams, jellies and mixed with other fruits in salads, pies and puddings. The berries are high in vitamin B. Teas and infusions of the

Above There are many types of sage, including one which smells of pineapple. The variety *Salvia officinalis* 'Purpurea' is shown here

Below Elder's dark, vitamin-rich berries provide the ingredient for jellies and wine, and the flowers for teas

Right The sweet-smelling cream umbels of elder, a welcome feature of our country lanes in May. Culpepper advised that the distilled waters of the flowers would relieve sores and ulcers on the skin

Below The young leaves of salad burnet taste of cucumber, but older foliage is bitter. Young leaves add flavour to salad dressings and to vegetables such as asparagus, chard and artichokes

flowers are used against colds. Flowers are used also in ointments, salves and lotions.

Sanguisorba minor
SALAD BURNET

This hardy perennial grows wild on chalky soil in many parts of the country. The little flowers appear at the end of long stalks in mid-summer, and are at first green and then open to show red styles. The attractive green foliage is cucumber-scented, lightly toothed and almost lacy in appearance. So hardy is this herb that it can sometimes continue to grow through winter. Plants will grow from 10cm–1m (4in–3ft) or so in height, depending on the depth and richness of the soil.

CULTIVATION Sow seed in spring in the open ground in ordinary soil. Divide roots in March or April. Give abundant water in dry seasons. If allowed to go to seed the plants will self-sow. Cut flower-ing stems from plants in order to obtain a good supply of fresh, green leaves.

USES One of the greatest benefits of salad burnet is that it holds its leaves through winter, thus providing a good source of materials to be used in winter salads. Its cucumber quality is also welcome in soups, stews and casseroles, as a garnish for many vegetable dishes and as an ingredient in butters and cheeses. In conjunction with mint it makes a good sauce for fish.

Satureja hortensis
SUMMER SAVORY

Known in Europe as the 'bean herb' because it is so frequently used with all types of this vegetable, summer savory is a useful annual, growing to about 60cm (2ft), with slim, pointed green leaves and tiny white or pinkish flowers enjoyed by bees. *Satureja montana* is the winter savory, a small, woody perennial with similar leaves which have less flavour.

CULTIVATION Sow seeds early enough in the year, May or June, for the leaves to be in season at the same time as bean crops. Ordinary soil and an open, sunny site is necessary. It grows well as a pot plant.

USES Summer savory has a spicy, almost peppery flavour, a little like a conjunction of thyme and mint. Yet used with almost any beans it loses its own personality and gives added flavour. It can also be used with soups and other vegetable dishes, sausages, meat pies and strong cheese dishes. One or two leaves, finely chopped, can go into a green salad to give an unexpected flavour.

Smyrnium olusatrum
ALEXANDERS

A biennial herb known and used in ancient times, it appears that the popular name Alexanders was given to it because it was much used during the reign of Alexander the Great. It grows up to about 1.5m (5ft), with broad, shining green leaves and umbels of yellow flowers. It is widely naturalised and grows particularly well near the sea. It was originally cultivated as a pot herb but became superseded by celery, the taste of which is similar and more effective.

CULTIVATION Sow seed in autumn in a sunny situation on light, well-drained soil. Transplant in spring when large enough to handle and gradually earth up to blanch the stems and leaves like celery as the plants grow.

USES The flavour of Alexanders is a little like celery though perhaps a bit more pungent. It can be boiled as a vegetable or the leaves and buds chopped to add to salads. As the stems are more highly flavoured, it is best to boil them, sometimes to flavour soups and stews.

Symphytum officinale
COMFREY

Comfrey is a large, spreading, easily grown perennial which will grow to more than 1m (3ft) tall and produce rough, hairy leaves 25cm (10in) long and purple, blue, pink or white flowers in drooping clusters throughout the summer. It has been well known and much used for centuries as a medicinal plant.

CULTIVATION Seed can be sown in autumn, but propagation by the division of roots at the same time is much easier. It grows easily, quickly and well in a moist, shady place such as the banks of a stream or ditch and, once established, it may become widely spread in its location. If allowed to seed in a garden it will become invasive, so flower stems should be removed as soon as they are past their best.

USES Comfrey can be used in a wide variety of medicinal forms and for a wide range of purposes. Teas are good for diseases of the lungs and should be freshly made as the liquid tends to ferment quickly. Ointments and poultices are used to treat wounds, abrasions, rheumatism and muscular complaints. Comfrey has achieved the common names of knitbone and noneset because poultices bandaged to broken bones are thought to aid in the speedy joining of the broken parts. The leaves can be used as a raw or cooked vegetable and are excellent in the preparation of garden compost. Roots are used to make pickles and for the brewing of a comfrey wine.

Left Also known as stonecrop, horse parsley, wild parsley and the black pot herb, Alexanders flowers in June and July. The stems were once used widely in soups and stews

Below Comfrey or knitbone is celebrated for its medicinal qualities, and is often applied as ointments or root poultices, or prepared as a tisane. The leaves can be cooked like spinach and eaten with eggs

Tanacetum vulgare
TANSY

A common wild plant, tansy is a hardy perennial with attractive 'bachelor's buttons' type of flowers — bright yellow, ray-less blooms in flat bunches. The plant will grow to about 1m (3ft) and has feathery, dark green, highly aromatic leaves. A variety *T.v. crispum* has finer foliage. It was once used as a strewing herb and moth repellent and even today is hung in bunches in some European doorways to keep out flies.

CULTIVATION Tansy has strong, creeping, even invasive roots that will grow almost anywhere. Plants are best grown by detaching these and planting them wherever they are needed.

USES Tansy has come under some suspicion as a culinary herb and is today used only as the ingredient for a tea or tisane which is said to be a tonic. It should not be taken too strong nor too frequently, but in any case the flavour is bitter and unpleasant. Flowers can be dried and used as perpetuelles. They and the leaves can be used also in potpourris.

Below The buttercup yellow, button blooms of tansy dry well for flower arrangements, and its leaves, used sparingly, can be added to custard. They are the essential ingredient of Tansy pudding

Thymus
THYME

Of the several score of *Thymus* species, all are said to derive from *T. serpyllum*, wild thyme, which, for this reason, is known as the mother of thyme. *T. vulgaris* is the garden thyme, the most aromatic and flavoursome, the most useful in the kitchen. There is, however, *T. citriodorus*, lemon thyme, with a distinct lemon scent and flavour, slightly milder than garden thyme. There are also several decorative forms, such as *T. vulgaris aurea* with striking golden leaves, which are attractive garden plants.

Thymus vulgaris grows wild on stony hillsides in Greece, where it has been known and used for centuries. It is a low-growing perennial shrub, evergreen, with small, highly aromatic leaves and pale purple flowers attractive to bees. Plants seldom grow to more than about 20cm (8in) tall and like a position in full sun in well-drained, though not necessarily stony soil, with some lime content. It may need protection during winter in cold, wet areas and like some other herbs, produces more flavour, more scent and greater value when grown in warm and sunny conditions.

CULTIVATION Propagation is by seeds sown in spring and by division in March or April. Plants should be replaced every three or four years as they become woody and straggling. Plants can be pot-grown indoors, in which case frequent cutting for culinary uses will provide bushy and attractive specimens.

USES This is one of the most important and useful culinary herbs, particularly suited to foods established in the areas where the plants grow best — the Mediterranean regions. Thyme goes well with richly flavoured meats, stews, pastas, with the olives and garlic and tomatoes so vital to dishes from those parts. It is an ingredient of bouquet garnis and many other herb mixtures.

Among other natural oils, thyme leaves contain thymol, a preservative, which adds to its value when used in the making of sausages, salamis, pâtés, cheeses and similar dishes that may be kept for long periods before use. The various medicinal uses include the preparation of teas, ointments, poultices, mouth washes and cosmetics.

Tropaeolum majus
NASTURTIUM

This is the familiar decorative hardy annual grown as climber and sprawler in gardens for the bright gold, orange and red trumpet flowers and the round, green, soft leaves. The plant first came from South America.

CULTIVATION Nasturtiums grow easily and will seed themselves once established. They produce the best flowers where the soil is poor and in full sun.

USES Nasturtiums are rich in vitamin C. Their leaves have a hot, peppery taste when chopped and added to a salad and they are used as an ingredient in sandwiches. They are a good substitute for watercress. The green seeds make a substitute for capers and again can be chopped and added to salads. Seeds and leaves, finely chopped, can be blended into butters and cheeses to give a deeper and more piquant flavour.

Urtica dioica
STINGING NETTLE

This soft, green perennial plant grows from 30cm–1.5m (1–5ft) tall. The toothed leaves and the stems on which they grow are covered with what appears to be soft hairs but which, when touched, are capable of injecting an immediate but brief-acting poison a producing a slight and irritating but quickly disappearing blister.

CULTIVATION Wherever the soil is rich and uncultivated nettles will grow. The roots, strong, fibrous, yellow and creeping, persist for years and unless restricted like mint will cover large areas. The leaves and the stems rot down each year to make a rich, moist, friable and productive soil.

USES Stinging nettles, far from being a mere garden nuisance, are a most useful and nutritional plant, and have been recognised as such for centuries. They contain several trace elements, vitamins, nitrogen and protein and can be boiled to make a spinach-like vegetable which is the base for an excellent soup; use the young shoots for this purpose.

Fibres from the stems can be used to make both cloth and paper. Plants are so rich in nitrogen that they are among the best subjects for making garden compost. They are also vital host plants for some of our most decorative butterflies. These prefer the young shoots, so cut down nettles in late summer ready for a late batch of eggs.

Leaves can be dried and rubbed to make a coarse powder which can be used as a flavouring and which at the same time provides minerals and natural salts.

Valeriana officinalis
VALERIAN, ALL-HEAL

A medium- to tall-growing perennial which will reach 1.5m (5ft), having bright green, divided and almost fern-like leaves and clusters of pale pink flowers. Valerian grows wild in ordinary soil in moist, shady places, usually where the ground is stony or well drained.

CULTIVATION Seeds are slow and uncertain to germinate, so division of the roots in March and April is the normal method of propagation. Plants do not seem to be particular about soil, but as they are comparatively large it is wise to allow plenty of space.

USES The name comes from the Latin *valere*, to be healthy. A nervine is produced from the plant which is said to induce sleep, which explains why valerian has long been known as a sedative and painkiller. However, infusions made from its roots should be taken with caution. Best perhaps to concentrate on its value as a linen herb and use it in potpourri and sachet mixtures. Cats are attracted by the scent of the root.

Above There are dwarf, as well as climbing varieties of nasturtium and these will grow happily in hanging baskets. The leaves are delicious in salads

CHAPTER SIX

HERBS FOR THE KITCHEN

Opposite The distinctive tastes of fresh herbs preserved in oils and vinegar are a valuable asset in the kitchen.

Below A savoury jelly based on apple and vinegar and flavoured with newly picked sprigs of rosemary

FOR MANY PEOPLE herbs are mainly associated with meat rather than with any other food and in this context some herbs are much more widely used than others. In this country, next to parsley, which appears to be used more for garnishes than for actual consumption (which is a pity since it is so rich in minerals), sage appears to be the most popular. It is widely sold in a dried form, even in butcher's shops, often mixed with other products to provide a 'convenient' stuffing for meats. Traditionally it is used with onions for pork, but it is also cooked with other meats, veal and chicken for instance, unfortunately often dominating them because its flavour can be so strong. Other popular and traditional meat and herb combinations are mint with lamb, horseradish with beef, parsley with ham and fish. Some cooks never vary these.

Obviously, as with all other foods, the preference for one herb rather than another is a matter of taste, but if no other herb is ever used, how do you make a choice or find a favourite? Certainly recipes are useful guides and there are reasons why traditions have been built up, but even these need to be tested and analysed, for what one cook may believe to be a too liberal use of a herb, another may find too frugal.

A point to bear in mind with all herbs is that just as freshness and drying have an influence on their flavour, so does heat. The strength of any herb, fresh or dried, may seem to increase when heated by cooking in comparison to the flavour when raw.

Rosemary

In my own case rosemary, a herb which some cookery writers warn their readers never to use excessively, has come to play an important role in many favourite dishes and is useful in minor ways. For instance, a full sprig thrown into a stock pan with chicken bones produces a pleasant aroma in the kitchen and also

Above Marjoram as a culinary herb has multiple uses. It has a powerful flavour, but if chopped finely may be added to robust soups. It is ideal for stuffings, and when spiked into roast lamb or beef enhances the meat considerably. The golden form is illustrated

Marjoram

Beef which is to be marinated will be made more tender and more flavoursome if marjoram is added to the marinade and to stews and casseroles. And spiced beef, which is studded with slivers of garlic, salted and rubbed with powdered mixed spices and allowed to rest for five days before being cooked in a covered pot with a 150ml (¼ pint) of water, will take on a finer flavour if a few sprays of marjoram and a dozen juniper berries are added to the ingredients.

To those who are used only to mint, marjoram imparts a new flavour to mutton or lamb, as does lemon balm.

Mint

The traditional mint sauce made with the chopped leaves, sugar and vinegar and served with lamb is an abomination to some, who feel that the vinegar and sugar spoil the flavour of the fine meat. For them, chopped mint mixed with garlic and scattered on the joint half way through the roasting, will flavour the meat deliciously and be much more acceptable.

Mint is very versatile. It goes surprisingly well with fish. It lends itself to sweet dishes. One simple way to use it attractively is to sprinkle it on pineapple, grapefruit, melon or Chinese gooseberries (Kiwi fruit) which are to be served as a first course. It is used with borage in fruit cups. It makes a delicious and refreshing sorbet.

MINT SORBET
Pick a good handful of mint, the round-leaved variety if possible, for this sweet.
  2 tsp powdered gelatine
  600ml (1 pint) water
  175g (6oz) sugar
  2 egg whites
  juice of half a lemon
  salt
Add the sugar to 450ml (¾ pint) of the water. Heat slowly until the sugar is dissolved, then bring to the boil and boil fairly rapidly for 10 minutes. Remove from the heat and add the chopped mint and lemon juice. Stir well and allow to steep for about one hour. Strain. Dissolve the gelatine in 150ml (¼ pint) of water, add to the syrup and mix well. Pour the syrup into a plastic container or into freezing trays and place in the freezer or

flavours the stock well. I use it also as a change from tarragon, for instance, when a chicken is to be roasted. Five centimetres (2in) or so of rosemary sprig is tucked between each wing and leg and the body. Alternatively, sometimes the leaves are cut small and mixed with chopped garlic or shallot and spread over the chicken breast, which has first been well moistened with lemon juice. In winter, when fresh basil is scarce, I use rosemary on pizzas and in tomato soups and sauces, for I find that, like basil, it goes very well with most vegetables. Use it also to bring a 'new' flavour to 'old' boiled potatoes.

The same method as that used for the roast chicken may be used when a joint of lamb is to be roasted, for rosemary and lamb, just as rosemary and kid and suckling pig, go excellently together. Rosemary, like thyme, can be mixed with other herbs. A shoulder or leg of lamb can be stuffed with a pungent mixture of rosemary, parsley, mint, garlic and lemon. Try rosemary instead of sage with pork, a favourite duo with Italian cooks. Use it also for some fish. Place a sprig on a steak of halibut or turbot before it goes under the grill. A great advantage is that rosemary can be picked the year round.

It can also be associated with milk puddings and cream dishes. Use a sprig in place of a bay leaf.

ice-making compartment of the refrigerator. When the syrup is partly set, bring it out and whisk it until it is opaque and much increased in bulk. Whisk the egg whites with a pinch of salt until they are stiff. Fold them into the beaten syrup. Blend well but carefully. Return to the freezer. To serve, shave off the sorbet with a metal spoon and heap the curls into cooled dishes. Just before serving decorate with crystallised mint.

MINT CHUTNEY
There are many recipes for mint in chutneys. One which is quick and easy, since no cooking is involved, is as follows:

    3 tbls chopped mint
    100g (4oz) sultanas
    100g (4oz) large raisins, chopped
    2 tbls tomato ketchup
    1 tbls brown sugar
    salt
    lemon juice
Blend the dried fruit and the mint. Stir in the sugar, ketchup, pinch of salt and about 1tsb lemon juice, adding more of this if the chutney seems not to be moist enough. Mix until all is well blended. Put into a covered jar. Store in the refrigerator.

Fennel

Fennel, whether the bulb-based Florence fennel or the common, leafy kind, need not be reserved for fish dishes. Its flavour provocatively complements roast pork and veal. Fennel seeds can be used in minced pork, ham, veal and sausage meat recipes.

Using Herbs with Yoghurt and Cheese

So far I have only touched on herb associations. It is inhibiting to think of certain herbs as being exclusive to certain foods, for most can be moved around successfully according to the cook's whim or intuition. My own rule is to use any herb which is in season or at hand rather than no herb at all. Keen cooks will find that an excellent source of inspiration are recipes from other countries. A search through their cook books almost always reveals other, unexpected ways of using a familiar herb.

For example, take the importance of yoghurt in the diet and cooking of many

Left Applemint, distinguishable by its round, pale green leaves and white hairy stems, is particularly good for mint sauce

countries where it is introduced into so many different kinds of dishes. Even served alone, laced with herbs, spices and certain vegetables such as cucumbers, it can provide a delicious supplement to many foods.

In this country, the present-day interest in whole and natural foods and diet has meant that yoghurt is in greater demand than it has ever been. As one might expect, here it is the sales of sweetened and fruit yoghurts which are highest, but the cook who is willing to experiment will find that natural or plain yoghurt is likely to be of the greatest benefit, for it is the perfect medium for herbs. For instance, salad dressings are made in seconds simply by adding chopped herbs, the kind selected being the one which, in the cook's opinion, would best complement the particular meat, fish, eggs, cheese or what ever is to be served with the salad. The herbs can also be mixed. They can be used in such quantity that the sauce itself is an appetising green and thick in texture, or the herbs can be sparse enough for the yoghurt to carry just a trace of the essential flavour.

Yoghurt cheese, a soft creamy cheese, simply made by letting yoghurt drip through a cheese cloth or white kitchen paper, is in Indian cookery mixed with herbs, in particular chives, coriander, dill, mint, parsley and tarragon, often with spring onions.

These are only a few of the ways yoghurt and herbs can help the enterprising cook. There are many others and a little research and experiment will prove most profitable.

Above Experimenting with different combinations of herbs is part of the fun of cooking with them. One danger, however, is that overuse of herbs may spoil the food. A rough guide is that one tablespoon of fresh, chopped herbs is satisfactory for a dish for four persons, but only half this amount should be added if the herbs you have are dried

Cottage cheese also is a bland food which can be greatly improved in flavour, and consequently more enjoyed, by the addition of herbs, a fact not lost on the manufacturers, who market cottage cheese with chives, a combination often served with jacket baked potato. But why not try chopped mint for a change?

Dieters who depend upon this cheese for sandwich fillings can make it much more tasty and nutritious by blending it with most other herbs, plain or mixed. Try also a mixture: tarragon and walnuts, parsley and cashews and other nut and herb mixtures. The contrast of textures is very pleasing and is one reason for using chopped fresh seeds of sweet cicely with its leaves.

Herb-flavoured Vinegars

Where vinaigrette or French dressings are preferred to creamy ones, these can be varied by using different herb-flavoured vinegars. Of these tarragon seems to be the most widely known, but many of the other herbs can also be used: bay, dill (the flower heads are best used for this), garlic, marjoram and thyme all make deliciously flavoured vinegars.

Mint is more often reserved for mint sauce, but it can be used for a vinegar.

TARRAGON VINEGAR

Gather a quantity of shoots of the herb. Lay them out thinly on a rack or on paper for three or four days so that they will wilt and lose much of their moisture content. Often flavour is strong in the stem of a leafy herb and worth conserving, but some cooks prefer to strip the leaves from the stems, an optional matter.

Have ready wide-mouthed preserving jars. Pack the shoots or the leaves into these. Cover them completely with white wine vinegar. Close and allow to stand for a week or so. Pour off a little of the vinegar so that it can be tested for aroma. If it does not seem strong enough allow all to stand a little longer. If too strong, add more vinegar. Finally, if you wish, strain off into bottles. Alternatively, leave it in the herb-filled jars to extract every drop of flavour.

HORSERADISH VINEGAR

This is made a little differently. Use 75g (3oz) of scraped or finely grated horse-radish to 1 litre (2 pints) of wine or cider vinegar. Add 25g (1oz) of finely minced shallot, one clove of garlic and 1tsp of cayenne pepper. Allow these to steep for a fortnight. Strain and bottle.

Herbs in Salads

Herbs can play such an important part in bringing variety and adding zest to salads. Take cucumber for instance, a popular salad vegetable whether served on its own or mixed with others, yet even a scattering of fresh chervil or mint leaves, torn rather than chopped, can transform its character. Try it with the following sauce:

DILL SAUCE
Into a jar pour 2 tbls of olive oil, 4 tbls lemon juice, 2 tbls fresh dill finely cut. Add salt and pepper to taste. Cover the jar tightly. Shake well so that all the ingredients blend well. Pour over sliced cucumber. Cover and chill.

Tomatoes both look and taste better if they are sprinkled with herbs. Even a little chopped shallot and parsley can make a world of difference. For a special occasion serve:

BRANDIED TOMATOES
Take six average-sized tomatoes and peel them carefully. Combine 150ml

(¼ pint) olive oil, ½ tsp salt, 1 tbls finely chopped parsley, 1 tbls finely chopped basil, 1 tsp finely grated lemon rind and 3tbls brandy. Pour the dressing over the tomatoes. Chill.

Olives and Herbs

Tinned or bottled olives and those which are vacuum-packed in bags, usually without oil and in brine, can be made much more delectable if they are drained where necessary, or simply removed from the pack, and transferred into herb-flavoured olive oil and allowed to marinate for at least a week or two before use.

Use a suitable sized jar. For a ½kg (1lb) size use two or three dried bay leaves and a dozen or so juniper berries (amounts

Left Apple-shaped cucumbers have an especially good flavour, which is enhanced by a dill sauce

Left Tarragon white wine vinegar flavoured with fresh leaves of the herb, makes a good salad dressing

are not critical, you must use your own judgement and taste) and two or three sprigs each of rosemary and thyme. If freshly picked these two should be dried in the air for a day or two before use. Dried bouquet garni sachets (see below) can also be used for this purpose. Completely cover all the herbs with olive oil. Allow to stand for at least a week. When some olives are subsequently removed from the jar, see that the contents remaining are still completely covered by the oil before closing the jar again. Add a little more oil if necessary. This way the olives will keep for a long time. The oil can be re-used for the same purpose as well as for salad dressings.

A less expensive oil, groundnut oil for instance, can be made to taste more like olive oil, and be more suitable for a salad dressing or mayonnaise, by using the same method. In this case, though, the olives and the herbs will improve the taste of the oil.

Using Bouquet Garni

Many recipes for many different kinds of foods and dishes call for the inclusion of a bouquet garni. This is the term given to a little bunch or bouquet of herbs. It may be small, medium or large, according to requirements, used to flavour sauces, stews, soups and sometimes casseroles and other prepared dishes as they cook.

Traditionally, parsley, thyme and bay are the basic herbs, usually tied together with a piece of long thread, one end of which is left outside the pan so that the bouquet can be pulled out when the cook feels that the dish has been flavoured sufficiently, or before serving.

There seems to be no real hard and fast rule about what the bouquet should include. Sometimes parsley alone is used. Sage is seldom used for a general purpose, although I like to use it with parsley and lovage and bay when I am boiling a bacon joint. So much depends upon the food to be flavoured and on the tastes and talents of the cook.

Not many readers nowadays will find themselves preparing turtle soup for which the traditional herbs are basil, marjoram, sorrel and thyme. However, you might keep these in mind as a flavouring for many clear soups other than turtle.

One excellent method of using herbs is to flavour the stock which is to be the base for a soup or a sauce. Chicken, pork, lamb, beef and other kinds of bones and fish, for instance, simmered for hours to

Below The traditional bouquet garni is a small bunch of fresh herbs, usually parsley, bay and thyme. These and other combinations of herbs may be used dried and secured in a muslin or cheesecloth bag which, once the cooking has finished, is removed from the pan

extract the greatest amount of goodness from them, can be given character by using the complementary herb or herbs and spices. Even sage comes into its own in this respect. Use it along with lemon balm and a sharp apple in stock made from ham bones.

Dried bouquet garni bags are popular. These are small pieces of muslin or cheese cloth, 7–10cm (3–4in) square, into which a small amount of mixed dried crushed herbs, usually about a level teaspoonful, is placed. The four corners of the cloth are then gathered up and the bundle tied with a long thread, the end of which is left free, again to facilitate removal from the pot.

Other Culinary Uses

In the main it is best to use fresh herbs as a garnish for soup rather than to introduce dried herbs into it as it is being prepared. Apart from the fact that the fresh flavour they contribute is incomparable to that of the dried leaves, the very appearance of finely chopped fresh green herbs floating on the surface of a bowl of soup is both attractive and stimulating to the taste buds. For both hot and chilled soups try a spoonful of herb-thick yoghurt or cream, or even cottage cheese, ladled into the centre on serving.

For those who do not eat meat the following recipe makes a very useful stock:

HERB BOUILLON OR STOCK
For 1 litre (2 pints) of water take 40g (1½oz) of fresh sorrel leaves with stems removed, 20g (¾oz) lettuce (a good use for the outside leaves), 14g (½oz) fresh chervil, 7g (¼oz) butter and salt according to taste or diet rules.

Cook the washed and de-stalked leaves until they are tender. Strain and discard the leaves. Add butter and salt to taste to the liquid.

If the herbs are to flavour a marinade for meat or fish, stronger herbs or a wider range may be called for, possibly with the addition of some spices. For instance, marjoram and basil may need to be included, espcially if later on in the preparation of the dish tomatoes or tomato juice may be used.

For a court bouillon in which such fish as pike or grey mullet are to be poached, suitable herbs include fennel, thyme and bay, all good fish herbs, along with parsley and parsley roots, or alternatively, parsnips, celery and such spices as dill, fennel and cumin seed and peppercorns. These should all be boiled together in the white wine or vinegar and water according to the recipe for about 20 minutes before the fish is introduced.

Herb Juices

Sometimes a bouillon, or maybe even a sauce made from all manner of good things, does not look as good as it tastes. Herb juices can be used not only to flavour it but also to colour it so that it looks more appetising. The usual herbs are chervil, parsley and tarragon; use just one or two if all three are not available. To these are added watercress, which provides an excellent deep green colour and an agreeable peppery taste. Nasturtium leaves make a satisfactory substitute for this.

Either pound all the herbs together in a mortar or use a food processor and then strain them. The process can be made easier in either case by adding a little of the stock or thin sauce to be coloured in the final stages. This makes it easier to strain the greenery. If the sauce or bouillon is to be served hot, blend in the juice at the last moment so that it keeps its colour.

Pot Herbs

Pot herbs are associated with soups and stews. These are not the same as the flavouring herbs, which will be needed in soups made from pot herbs anyway. Pot herbs are those vegetables, leafy and root kinds, which are traditionally used in stews and soups, mainly carrots, swedes, turnips, parsnips and celery. In French cookery they are more likely to be lettuce, orach, seakale, sorrel and spinach and Swiss chard.

Preparing Herb Sauces

There are a few classic sauces in which herbs play an important part:

ESCOFFIER MAYONNAISE
This sauce is usually served with cold roast beef. It is also excellent with cold salmon and other fish. However, vegetarians will find it excellent with a rice salad and other fairly bland basic foods.

It is made by adding freshly grated horse-radish, chopped parsley and chopped chervil to the mayonnaise. Mix in a little to begin with and taste for flavour. The sauce should be piquante.

REMOULADE SAUCE

Obviously the mayonnaise is a base on which one can play many variations. Remoulade is another classic. To the mayonnaise is added a mixture of finely chopped chervil, parsley and tarragon, along with spring onions, including a portion of their green stems, gherkins and capers, laced with pounded anchovies.

PESTO SAUCE

Those who enjoy Italian food will know how highly regarded is the Genoese sauce *Pesto*, which is served, uncooked and unheated, with various kinds of pastas and gnocchi and in minestrone and some other soups. An imaginative cook will soon devise other ways of serving this delicious concoction, for example with jacket baked potatoes instead of the usual cream cheese and chives, or blended into yoghurt as a dressing for a potato salad.

In Italy pesto is often made in sufficient quantities to store. It is packed firmly into jars and the surface covered with a good layer of olive oil.

To serve six people, take 50g (2oz) fresh basil leaves (dried basil will not do) plucked from their stems, 25g (1oz) pinoli or pine nuts, 25g (1oz) grated Parmesan cheese, 50g (2oz) olive oil, 2 cloves of garlic and a little salt.

Pound the basil, pinoli, garlic and a little salt to a puree. Alternatively, use a food processor. Add the cheese. Begin adding olive oil to the puree in much the same way as you would make a mayonnaise. Continue until the pesto reaches the consistency of a very thick mayonnaise.

Sometimes parsley and marjoram together are used as a substitute for basil. The resulting sauce is not so distinctive in flavour, but on the other hand it is another good herb sauce and one which is worth trying.

Omelette

Herbs and omelettes have a natural affinity. *Omelettes aux Fines Herbes* is one of the world's great dishes, but only those who use herbs liberally are really likely to make it as it should be served. Larousse comments severely that 'usually and quite wrongly, this omelette is prepared by adding only chopped parsley to the eggs. Actually omelette aux fines herbes should contain chopped parsley, chervil, tarragon and even spring onions or chives and there must be enough of all these aromatic herbs to make the omelette green.' Good advice, which could profitably be followed for so many other dishes. A herb-green spaghetti is most delectable. Herb butters should also contain plenty of green colour.

Herb Butters

Use these to add zest to simple meals. Hot scones and herb butter can be as delicious in their own way as hot scones and strawberry jam and cream. Herb butters can easily be frozen, so it may be worthwhile making a large quantity. Margarine can be flavoured and coloured in the same way.

Chop or process the herbs finely. Mix in the ratio of 1 heaped tsp of herbs (at least) to 50g (2oz) butter. Blend them together with a palette knife and pat into shape. Large quantities are easily made in a food processor.

Prepare small quantities or pats for certain dishes, say parsley, chervil or fennel for fish, marjoram for steaks, tarragon for chicken, basil for broad beans, according to your taste or fancy.

Herb Sweets

These are not to be confused with 'sweet herbs', the old name given to sweet-smelling strewing herbs and those kinds used in potpourris and other mainly non-edible products, which are described more fully in the following chapter. Included are those herbs which can be used in sweet dishes of various kinds, preserves, wines and confectionary.

Probably the best known of these is angelica, the sweet, thick stems of which are divided into sections and candied. In commerce these are taken from three-year-old plants which have been prevented from flowering and thus encouraged to become perennial, sending up a thicker stem each year. The old method of candying can be a very lengthy process, which is probably the reason why more people buy candied

angelica than make it themselves. However one modern method offers a comparatively short process. Incidentally, the stems do not have to come from three-year-old plants, but instead may be taken from those of the current year. Fat leaf stalks may also be used — in which case a slimmer version of the commercial candy is produced, yet in some ways cooks may find this more convenient to use. Apart from using candied angelica in and on cakes and trifles, scatter small pieces as a garnish on a fruit salad and, mainly for appearance, on white or pale

fruits such as pears, lychees and apples.

Cut the tall stems down before the plant flowers and use them fresh. Early summer is usually the best time to harvest the stems.

CANDIED ANGELICA

Cut all the stems into sections some 8–10cm (3–4in) in length. Use a large pan and just cover the stems with water. Simmer until tender; test by squeezing a stem. Drain thoroughly. Weigh and place the angelica in a bowl and cover it with an equal amount in weight of sugar. Cover

Above Herb butters not only enliven a simple meal but they look attractive too. The finely chopped herbs are beaten into softened and salted butter which may be sharpened with a little lemon juice

Above Candied angelica is made from the young stems and the fleshy leaf stalks of the herb. Crystallised angelica can be stored though it will not keep so long as commercially prepared stems

Right Crystallised rose petals can be used as an original and colourful cake decoration or included in a sorbet

and allow to stand for two days. Transfer all to a preserving pan. Bring slowly to the boil, then simmer again very slowly until the angelica is translucent, when it should also be a very pleasant green in colour. Drain well. Dip or roll each stem in caster sugar until it is well coated. Place in single layers, each stem well spaced, on cake racks or on sheets of waxed paper to dry in the air or in a cool oven. Turn the stems from time to time. When the candy comes away from the rack or paper easily and feels dry to the touch, store it in covered jars. The syrup may be used as a base for fruit salads. A tablespoonful should sweeten and flavour sufficient fruit salad for four to six people, but this is a matter of taste. It keeps well in a covered jar.

Angelica has the effect of lessening acidity in both rhubarb and gooseberries; actually it would be worth trying on some other fruits where the season coincides, early cooking apples for instance. Add pieces of raw stem to these two when they are ready for cooking. Some cooks say that the angelica improves the flavour also. Where rhubarb or gooseberries are used in puddings or some similar dish, the addition of some candied angelica, either as a decoration or as an ingredient, will add to its appearance.

Like sweet cicely, which is closely related, angelica is versatile. The stems of both herbs are good to eat raw, although sometimes a little tough. The roots also are edible. The seeds have a pleasant flavour and can be used in salads.

CRYSTALLISED LEAVES AND FLOWERS

When used for cake or pudding decoration it is possible to make an entire 'rose' from rose petals, or to fashion a garland of violets or blue borage around the edge of a cake. Crystallised mint leaves will add attraction to a sorbet, but these should be added at the last minute so that the dishes come to table looking crisp and beautiful. Avoid bruising the subjects to be treated as this may discolour them. Using a pastry brush, paint both surfaces of the leaves or petals with beaten egg white. Have ready some waxed paper on which caster sugar has been sifted. As each piece is painted lay it, and press it lightly if necessary, on the sugar layer so that the underside becomes coated. Sift a little more sugar on the upper surface, enough to coat it well. When all are coated with sugar, dry them in a slow oven, turning them from time to time. To store, pack between waxed paper in an airtight container.

Herb Sugars

Rosemary and lavender sugars can be used to flavour custards, junkets, milk and cream desserts and puddings. Scented geranium leaves, lemon and rose scented particularly, can be used to flavour sugars for sponge cakes and puddings. The process is roughly the same for all.

ROSEMARY SUGAR

Take several full sprigs of clean rosemary. Pack them, standing, in a deep, screw-top jar. Pour in enough caster sugar to cover the herbs completely, leaving at least an inch of headroom. Close the jar and shake it vigorously. Let it stand for 24 hours and shake it well again. Allow it to stand for two weeks or so and then remove the lid and test for scent. When this is strong enough remove the rosemary. Keep the jar closed when the sugar is not in use.

Cooking with Flowers

Like some other daisies, the pot marigold, *Calendula officinalis*, has its culinary uses. Fresh, whole or chopped petals can be used to colour a salad or a rice dish. The petals, which retain their colour when dried, are sometimes used as an adulterant or even a substitute for saffron, which is the stamens of a crocus species. Dried, they were once used extensively in many European countries as a colouring and flavouring for soups. The petals, dried or fresh, can be pounded and blended in custards and creams. For the former, measure them first by bulk, loosely packed, and use equal quantities of petals and milk. The marigold flavour suits apples, pears and quince, so they can be combined with any of these fruits in savoury or sweet puddings and other desserts.

MARIGOLD CUSTARDS

Petals from 12 marigolds. More, according to taste, can be used, the limit being 570ml (1 pint) of petals to 570ml (1 pint) of milk. It is best to experiment. If dried petals are to be used, soak them in milk until they become soft, perhaps overnight.

    570ml (1 pint) of milk
    2 eggs
    1 dessertspoonful of sugar
    6 ramekins or small oven dishes

Pound the petals and sugar together (a food processor can be used for this and for the entire preparation) until an orange-coloured pulp is produced. Beat the eggs into the milk. Add this mixture to the flower pulp. Stir all together until well blended. Arrange six ramekin dishes in a roasting tin, not quite touching each other. Divide the mixture between them. Pour hot water into the

Below Individually baked custards, to be served as starters or desserts, can be flavoured with various herbs and flower petals. This unusual sweet is made from marigold petals

tin so that it reaches to 13mm (½in) or so below the rims. Bake at in a cool oven for 45 minutes or until the custards are set. The custards can be served hot or cold.

Herb-flavoured Jellies

Apple, rhubarb, grape, lemon, red and white currant, gooseberry, quince and other fruit juices can be used as a base for herb-flavoured jellies to serve with game and other meats, either hot or cold. A spoonful or two can also be stirred into gravy or sauces. It is best to use fresh herbs. If dried herbs are to be used tie them up in a muslin cloth. Basil, marjoram, rosemary, sage, tarragon, thyme and mint are most often used.

BASIC RECIPE
To each 600ml (1 pint) of juice, gained by simmering the fruit until tender in just enough water to float them and then straining through a jelly bag, use a really good bunch of the herb. Simmer this in the juice until the liquid is well flavoured. Remove the herb. Measure the liquid. Allow 450g (1lb) sugar to 600ml (1 pint). Boil the two together until the liquid sets when tested. Pour into warm jars and seal at once.

For a lemon jelly base first wash the lemons well (they may have been sprayed with chemicals at some time), cut them into quarters, remove the pips, put the quarters in a large bowl, barely cover with water and allow to stand overnight. Bring to the boil and allow to simmer briskly for two hours. Strain through a jelly bag. Measure the juice and allow 450g (1lb) sugar to each pint. Stir well. Boil until the jelly sets when tested. The lemon taste can be emphasised by boiling verbena leaves, two to each 300ml (½pint), in the liquid. Remove before potting. This base particularly suits sage, thyme, basil and savory.

HERB AND RHUBARB JELLY
The basic idea is the same as above but the method of preparation is a little different. First prepare the juice by stewing the cut rhubarb stems in enough water to float them. When they are tender and the water well coloured, strain them carefully to produce about 150ml (¼ pint) of thick juice. Add the juice of two lemons. Have ready the herb to be jellied, coarsely chopped in a bowl. Pour 600ml (1 pint) boiling water over it. Allow this infusion to stand for at least 30 minutes.

Strain and discard the herbs. Add more water if necessary to bring the level up to 600ml (1 pint) again. Add the fruit juice and 570g (1¼lb) sugar. Bring to the boil and allow to continue to boil fast until the jelly sets when tested. Pour into hot jars, cover when cool.

PARSLEY JELLY
This follows a different recipe. Wash the parsley well. Put it into a preserving pan with sufficient water to cover it. Bring to the boil, simmer for 15 minutes and then strain. Measure the juice. To every 600ml (1 pint) add 450g (1lb) of sugar and the juice of a lemon. Bring all to the boil and continue to boil fast until it forms a jelly.

Herb Teas, Tisanes and Wines

Herb teas, once widely used, some as refreshing drinks, others for minor ailments, are enjoying a revival. Sage and labrador teas are sipped for coughs, peppermint and lovage taken as restoratives, dill, fennel and caraway among many others to help the digestion, catmint to soothe and, like parsley, also to act as a febrifuge, chamomile as a guard against sleeplessness, and others such as balm and bergamot leaves, elder, jasmine, lime, woodruff flowers and rose petals simply because they make a delicious — and if you grow your own — an inexpensive drink.

Most are taken hot like ordinary tea, sometimes sweetened. Simply steep the dried leaves or flowers in boiling water and allow to brew for about five minutes, then strain and sip.

In a few cases, chamomile is an example, the flowers are boiled in a covered saucepan for half a minute and then left to brew like the others.

Both woodruff and bergamot, which is also known as Oswego tea, can be mixed when dried with either Indian or China tea, an economy practised when the more expensive real teas were introduced. These two are excellent when served ice cold.

As well as tisanes, some herbs can be made into country wines and other refreshing drinks. Surprisingly, perhaps, parsley wine is extraordinarily good and it is quite easy to make. Modern yeast tablets will be used today instead of the old toast and yeast method which is given here because it was the original.

PARSLEY WINE

450g (1lb) parsley
4.5 litres (1gal) boiling water
25g (1oz) lump ginger
2 oranges
2 lemons
1.8kg (4lb) sugar
14g (½oz) yeast, slice of toast

Place the parsley in a large bowl and pour on the boiling water. Allow all to steep for 24 hours, then strain. Boil the liquor with the ginger and the rinds of the oranges and lemons. Have ready the orange and lemon juice in a large bowl or jar. Pour the parsley liquid on to this. When nearly cool add the yeast spread on a piece of toast. Cover with a cloth and allow to stand for four days. Strain and pour into jars or bottles fitted with air locks. Cork when all fermentation has ceased.

ROSE PETAL WINE

Sweet scented roses make delicious wines, the colours of which vary according to the colour of the rose petals. One made from Albertine, a climbing variety which produces flowers in great abundance, resembles a Rhine wine.

For every 2.75 litres (5 pints) of petals you will need:

1kg (2¼lb) sugar
2.75 litres (5 pints) water
Juice and peel of 1 lemon
28g (1oz) yeast, or alternatively, a
    yeast tablet.

The citrus peel must be thinly pared as pith makes the wine bitter. Bring the water to the boil and pour it over the petals in a large bowl. Cover with a cloth. Allow to infuse for 72 hours, stirring twice daily. Strain through a non-metal sieve or muslin into a preserving pan. Squeeze the petals as dry as possible. Add the thin citrus peels. Bring to the boil, then simmer for 15–20 minutes.

Have ready a 4.5 litre (1 gallon) fermentation jar into which the sugar has been poured. Stand this on a board and pour in the hot rose liquid. Shake the vessel to dissolve the sugar. Plug the neck of the jar with sterile cotton wool. Leave to cool to blood heat. Add the citrus juices and the yeast. When cool fit an air lock into the neck of the jar. After the first rapid fermentation has ceased, top up the level with tap water. Allow the liquid to continue to ferment gently until the wine is clear and no longer bubbles; this usually takes from three to eight months. Syphon into sterilised bottles. Cork and seal.

RHUBARD AND BALM WINE

This can be drunk the same day that it is made:

900g (2lb) rhubarb
225g (½lb) balm leaves
4.5 litres (1gal) water
14g (½oz) yeast
14g (½oz) citric acid
450–680g (1–1½lb) demerara sugar,
    according to taste

Clean the rhubarb and balm leaves. Cut the rhubarb stems into sections. Put both in a preserving pan with the cold water. Bring to the boil and allow it to continue boiling for 30 minutes. Strain into a bowl or jar (not metal). When lukewarm add the yeast, citric acid and the sugar. Cover with a cloth. Allow it all to ferment for 24 hours. Skim and bottle.

Above Wines can be made from many flowers including broom, cowslip, elder, clover and dandelion. Fermented rose petals will produce a light, fragrant wine

HERBS FOR HEALTH AND BEAUTY

Opposite The pale pink blooms of the hybrid musk rose 'Penelope' provide successive supplies of highly scented petals for the amateur perfume maker

THROUGHOUT THE WORLD for centuries people have turned to plants, not only to help them comfort bruised bodies, staunch blood, clean wounds, restore spirits and even, or so they believed, prolong both youth and life, but also they have sought and found diverse ways and means of capturing and preserving the sweet scents. Inevitably, some plants have come to be more highly regarded than others for this purpose and, surprisingly perhaps, these are not always those which when fresh and at their peak are very sweet scented, for often their perfume cannot be extracted in any way. Lilies are an example.

Roses have always been great favourites, and of these it is some of the species and old-fashioned varieties which have the strongest perfume. Many modern

roses seem to have no discernible scent when fresh. However, I have discovered that some of these do become very scented when dried, so it would pay the rose grower to test any of these kinds if petals are required for potpourri or for some similar product.

The sources for 'flower' perfumes vary and not all come from the actual flower, for there is scented bark, as in cinnamon, scented seeds as in many spices and the seed pod of the vanilla orchid, scented roots as in the Florentine iris, angelica, sweet cicely and *Geranium macrorrhizum*, and many, many leaves.

On a large scale, different ways have been found of extracting the scented oils from some flowers and leaves and of distilling them to make and market perfumes, a process which has become vastly commercial throughout the world and upon which some areas, Grasse in Provence for example, have become dependent, for here scent is the local industry.

The production of scent is now generally much too complicated for the amateur to hope to emulate, but there still exist the original methods of capturing the scent of flowers which can be followed at home. In some ways home-made scents have an advantage over those which are commercially produced because they will be true flower scents, no substitutes will be used as they are in industry. Their manufacture is not only much easier but also in its way much more enjoyable and, when successful, so very satisfying. How delightful, for instance, on a hot, dusty, tiring day to bathe your hands or face in water scented by a home-made eau de toilette, or to apply a cooling lotion made soothing by fragrant herbs growing there

Right These stylised but exact illustrations of cinnamon, nard, balsam and valerian, originating from a twelfth century Persian manuscript, show that early perfumers, like apothecaries, were well acquainted with the plants they considered useful for their trade

Le Livre des Parfums   *Chap. III*

LES PRINCIPAUX PARFUMS DES HEBREUX
D'APRÈS UN MANUSCRIT ARABE PERSAN DU 12ème SIÈCLE

in the garden, or on a winter's night to slip down between sheets scented with lavender harvested in summer and redolent still of bright warm, sunny days.

Lavender

Few flowers scent the air as strongly as lavender does. To walk near its bushes in a garden or to drive through a country area where it is being grown commercially, or, as in some Mediterranean regions, where it grows wild, is to breathe perfume. The drier the air and the hotter the sun, the more quickly does the plant release its volatile oils to the air. This is why it is best to gather lavender early in the day, while its qualities are still conserved. If the flowers are wet with dew or rain, make a good bunch and swish it back and forth until no more water is thrown off. Cut each stem as long as possible, right down to where the leaves grow, actually taking a few of these with the stem and stripping them off later. Save the leaves for making potpourri or lavender water. This is also an excellent way of keeping the bushes neatly pruned.

Either make the stems into small bunches, tied tightly to allow for shrinkage, and hang them head downwards in a cool, airy place out of the sun, or alternatively, in the same kind of atmosphere, lay the stems out to dry on newspaper or

on a rack or table made from wire netting, which allows the air to circulate all round the stems. Do not make deep layers or the flowers might become mouldy.

LAVENDER BOTTLES

These are made to be laid among linen. They are always appealing and are very acceptable little gifts. Your first bottle may not look very sleek, but the results will improve with a little practice. Sometimes I make a variation on the lavender bottle, turning it into a 'scent' bottle by tying inside it other scented sprigs, southernwood and eau de cologne mint, for instance.

The lavender stems should be freshly picked so that they are supple. Take eleven stems of lavender, or a greater odd number, and about 1m (3ft) of ribbon. Bunch the flowers with the base of their heads level. Tie the ribbon at this point, leaving a long end which is to be woven through the stems. To do this, hold the bunch in one hand and gently bend each stem just below the tie, taking it right down over the flower spike. Bring the long length of ribbon through to what will now be the outside of the bottle and bend all the other stems the same way so that the flower heads are inside a cage of stems.

They now have to be more closely caged. To do this, weave the ribbon in and out of the stems. Take it and pass it over the first stem and under the next, keeping the ribbon flat all the time. Go on, round and round, keeping the ribbon flat and its edges touching until it is all used or until as much of the 'bottle' as you wish is covered. Stitch the ribbon end in place. Cover this area with a little ribbon bow.

Fix a small strip of ribbon lower down the stems to hold them in place. See that they all lie straight. Trim and/or shorten the ends to make them level.

LAVENDER WATER

This is made by using both the flowers and the leaves. Quantities are not critical and both fresh and dried material, together or separate, can be used. For instance, if you have only a small amount of dried lavender flowers, you can increase this by adding fresh leaves.

Measure a 300ml (½ pint) of lavender, fairly well packed, and boil it in just enough water to cover it. Clean rainwater is best but not essential for this. Let all simmer for 15 minutes and then allow to

Below Lavender bound into 'bottles' with ribbon form ideal objects for keeping linen smelling fresh and clean

cool and steep for at least an hour. Strain. The lavender water is now ready to use, but in this state it cannot be kept for long. To preserve it, and at the same time to provide a fixative for the scent, add a teaspoon of pure alcohol, vodka or brandy. Bottle and close the top.

LAVENDER BAGS

These are filled with lavender flowers, but you can also add dried leaves, although these are not strongly scented enough to use alone. Strip the flowers from the stems (save the stems to burn like incense to sweeten the air in a close room). Make sure that they are completely dry. Keep them in airtight containers until you are ready to use them. Lavender flowers when properly dried should keep their fragrance for five years or so.

Make the bags from small double squares or other shaped pieces of muslin or some very fine cotton material. A purple- or lavender-coloured pattern adds to the charm of the finished bags as does a touch of lavender-coloured ribbon or stitching. Obviously, the bags are left open at one end for filling. Later they are either stitched so that the bag lies flat when filled, suitable for placing among linen sheets and similar items, or the neck of the bag can be drawn up so that the lavender is in a little sack. Gathered prettily and given a little loop, this kind can be hung from a coat hanger.

The same pattern of hanging bag can be used for moth-repellent mixtures.

LAVENDER POTPOURRI

This is one of the simplest of all potpourri recipes. To each 225g (8oz) of stripped lavender flowers add 15g (½oz) dried thyme flowers and leaves, 15g (½oz) scented mint leaves, 7g (¼oz) powdered cloves, 7g (¼oz) powdered caraway seed and 25g (1oz) coarse sea salt. Mix well. When this is left about the house in bowls, stir the contents from time to time to release the scents.

POTPOURRI

Those who have once made potpourri successfully are most likely never to be without it again. Not all potpourris are made quite so quickly and simply as the one just described, but none is difficult.

Many potpourri flowers have colours which tend to fade when the petals dry. Some of the unscented or lesser scented

kinds retain their colours and for this reason are worth including simply to make the potpourri mixture more appealing to the eye. Pot geranium (pelargonium) petals, for instance, keep their colours well, so collect and keep any which fall from the pots on the windowsill. Some varieties have flower clusters which conveniently dry whole on the plant and so are little trouble to collect. Delphinium florets bring a pleasant and often complementary blue to petal mixtures and so do borage flowers. Experiment with others, but only use enough to add a little colour. If the potpourri is to be used as a gift and is to be packed in a transparent box, press some flowers to decorate the surface, heartsease, geranium and single stocks, for instance.

As might be expected, potpourri scents vary according to the ingredients. One made mostly of rose petals will differ from one made of philadelphus, lavender, marigolds or verbena. The charm of potpourri is that one scent seldom dominates. It will be there, but only scarcely definable.

Although in recipes quantities are usually given, these are not critical as they might be in a cooking recipe. Take the recipe as a guide and use what flowers are available or can be spared. To eke out the flowers, fragrant leaves

Above The long lasting but pleasantly refreshing aroma of lavender can also be harnessed in a potpourri – a handful of dried flowers placed in an open bowl or bag, and left to perfume the room

can be used generously. These, like flowers, should be picked fresh and dried quickly. They include balm, lemon and other thymes, variegated and other scented mints, verbena or lippia, sweet chamomile, cistus, tutsan, sweet briar rose, tansy and the scented-leaved pelargoniums. You need not pick fresh leaves of the last, for the faded leaves on the base of the stems of a growing plant are always very scented.

In the main, recipes are divided into two kinds, wet and dry potpourri. The first term is somewhat misleading, for it conjures up a watery image, which is incorrect. The description is a very loose one and 'bowl' potpourri might be better, for this is the kind which traditionally is placed about the home in perforated china pots and bowls made specially to hold the mixture and at the same time to release its scent slowly into the atmosphere. This is not the best kind to use for filling sachets, bags and pillows. For these, potpourri made by following the 'dry' method is best. It is much more adaptable and can be used with a greater variety of ingredients.

To retain their strength flower scents must be fixed. The ingredients for use as fixatives vary. Coarse, that is, sea, sometimes called bay salt is one. Another is dried and powdered citrus peel. Dry orange, tangerine and lemon peel in a cool oven, or keep them in a warm, dry place until they are hard enough to be ground or pounded to a powder. I use an electric coffee grinder for this. Store the powder in covered jars. I use roughly 1 teaspoonful of the fixative to 1 litre (2 pints) of flower petals or to a flower and leaf mixture. Orris root, a scented fixative, is available from some chemist shops, some health food stores and some herbalists. Angelica and sweet cicely root powders can also be used. Talcum powder is a good alternative. There are also certain exotic gums and essential oils, but these add to both the cost and the complexity of the potpourri without conferring any vital benefits. Some of the sweetly aromatic spices can also be added to vary the scents.

You can make a basic spice mixture and store it in an airtight jar ready for use. Spice mixtures vary from just cinnamon and cloves to those which include gums and oils. The latter are sometimes on sale in Indian shops or from herbalists. You can also often find such treasures when you are abroad on holiday.

SPICE MIXTURE
Take 25g (1oz) each benzoin, angelica root, cloves, powdered nutmeg, powdered cinnamon and oil of bergamot, 50g (2oz) powdered orris root, 1 level tsp powdered lemon rind, and — although this is optional — a few drops of oil of musk, also called musk ambrettes. Mix all together.

Bowl potpourri

To make bowl or 'wet' potpourri, fresh or half-dried (hence the term 'wet') petals and leaves are placed in layers about 5cm (2in) deep inside a glass jar. The layers are sprinkled with spices — allspice and cloves are the two main spices used in this kind of potpourri — and then covered with common sea or bay salt which is sprinkled on thickly enough to cover petals and leaves completely. As a preservative, brandy, vodka, Polish spirit or pure alcohol is also sometimes sprinkled over each layer.

These bowl mixtures are very long-lasting when properly made, but on the whole I find 'dry' potpourri mixtures are more successful and certainly more adaptable.

Basic Dry Potpourri

For this it is a good plan to have ready a good fragrant leaf mixture. Keep it tightly sealed until required. Meanwhile the stock of flowers can gradually be built up. These can be all of one kind or mixed.

To 1 litre (2 pints) of dried flowers add 250g (9oz) of leaves, 50g (2oz) of coarse salt, ½ tsp citrus peel, 7g (¼oz) each of orris root and cinnamon and a good pinch of nutmeg, cloves, allspice and sandalwood.

Pour all the ingredients into a canister or large jar which can be tightly covered. Stir the contents each day, covering closely again each time. When the contents begin to smell really strongly sweet, usually after a week or two, the potpourri can be used to fill bowls or bags.

The suggested spices are not critical and it is worth experimenting. Often a different spice proves more appealing, ground coriander for instance, ground dried angelica or sweet cicely seeds, even fennel, can contribute an elusive and engaging aroma.

There exists great scope for trial and experiment when making potpourris. The following recipes may guide those who are interested even further:

ROSE AND VANILLA POTPOURRI
This is a compromise, for it borrows something from the old 'wet' or bowl method in the way the ingredients are assembled, but thoroughly dried, not half-dried, petals are used.

Take two vanilla pods, 1–1.5 litres (2–3 pints) of dried rose petals, 50g (2oz) orris root, 25g (1oz) sandalwood powder, 1tsp cinnamon powder, 50g (2oz) coarse sea salt.

Mix the spices well. Stand the vanilla pods upright inside a storage jar. Put the rose petals in 5cm (2in) deep layers and cover each layer first with a sprinkling of mixed spices and then a deeper layer of salt. Cover the jar tightly. Store for at

Below The ingredients of potpourri may be varied considerably and can include fruits, bark and leaves besides flowers. Each recipe, however, should have a main scent and a fixative such as orris root or dried citrus peel that will preserve the aromatic properties

least one month before putting the pot-pourri into jars or sachets. The vanilla pods can be removed and used time and time again.

LEMON-YELLOW POTPOURRI

This, one of my own concoctions, was made because very early one spring a bowl of yellow freesias yielded a generous quantity of flowers which dried on the stems. These were pulled off daily to encourage the buds at the top of the stem to open. Then came winter jasmine, which also dries well on the stem in a vase, but which does not, like its white-flowered relations, have any perfume. However, these two gave a good basis on which to begin collecting. As the year passed they were joined by wallflowers, and through the summer various kinds of marigolds, yellow rose petals, santolina and curry plant flowers. Yellow pansies were pressed to scatter on the surface.

To 250ml (9fl oz), fairly well packed, of yellow petals and/or flowers add 750ml (1¼ pints) of dried leaves, which should include balm, cistus, lemon thyme, verbena or lippia and lemon-scented pelargonium, ½ tsp powdered lemon peel, 25g (1oz) orris, angelica or sweet cicely root, 6 drops of lemon verbena oil or citronella.

Mix all together well. Use for bowls or sachets.

A POTPOURRI FOR LINEN

750ml (1¼ pints) dried philadelphus blossom, 250ml (9fl oz) dried rose geranium, *Pelargonium graveolens* and *P. capitatum* leaves, 1tsp powdered angelica root or any of the other roots.

Mix all together well. Make and fill little bags so that the potpourri can be laid among linen.

GERANIUM SWEET BAG MIXTURE

Use roughly equal quantities of leaves from potted scented pelargoniums and hardy geraniums such as *G. macrorrhizum*. When these are dried rub them to a rough powder. To them add an equal quantity of powdered lavender. To each 250ml (9fl oz) of this leaf and flower mixture add a heaped teaspoon of orris root powder. Use the mixture to fill small muslin bags.

POMANDERS

Modern pomanders are usually made from oranges studded with cloves, but you can also use any long-lasting apple for the same purpose. In fact, I prefer pomanders made from Bramley apples to those made from oranges because the scent of the apples seems sweeter and longer lasting.

For a medium-sized fruit you will need about 28g (1oz) of cloves. You need also a teaspoon of powdered cinnamon and orris root, 30cm (1ft) or so of narrow tape, some slightly narrower ribbon to replace the tape (which becomes soiled while the studded fruit is drying), a few pins, and a cocktail stick to help pierce the skin of the fruit should this be tough.

Use the tape to divide the circumference of the fruit into four equal sections. Pin one end to the top of the fruit. Pass the tape right round in one direction, pinning it in place again at the opposite pole. Pass another length of tape around the fruit in the other direction so that the tapes cross at the two poles.

Press the stalks of the cloves into the fruit, following at first the edges of the tapes, then gradually working towards the middle of each of the four sections.

When the fruit is completely covered with the tightly packed cloves, roll it in the spice mixture; this is most easily done if the spices are placed in a small bag. Make sure that the fruit is well dusted with the spices. The fruit can be left in the bag (leaving the top open if it is made of plastic) and placed in an airing cupboard or some dry, dark place to dry.

Below A bramley apple pomander. Originally mixtures of herbs and spices were carried to ward off infections thought to be spread on the wind. Pomanders today are used to deter moths and to leave pleasant aromas in cupboards and drawers

Remove the tape after about two weeks so that the skin under it can dry properly. When the pomander feels dry, decorate it with ribbon where the tape once was, pinning this into place. The pin will rust and hold fast.

BATH BAGS
Dry and mix thoroughly in equal quantities lemon balm, rosemary, lavender leaves or flower spikes, eau de cologne and pineapple mint, philadelphus flowers, lime flowers, or failing these, whatever else is available, but all if possible.

Make small bags or sachets of muslin or fine net, fill with the mixture and fasten. Throw the bags into a hot bath to scent the bath water.

SLEEP PILLOWS
Since drinking beer makes some people sleepy, it is not surprising that hops, the herb from which beer is brewed, also have a soporific effect. Pillows stuffed with dried hops and placed so that they lie literally beneath one's nose, have long been recommended as a cure for insomnia. Hops may be used alone, but they are more often mixed with one, or several, of the following: lavender, verbena, marjoram and peppermint and/or dried flowers of various kinds, in particular mignonette, rose, meadowsweet, honeysuckle, lady's bedstraw and chamomile.

Enclosed in a thin fabric case, a stuffing of this kind can be uncomfortable and the contents often rustle too much for perfect peace. To suppress the latter it is recommended that before using them the hops be softened by sprinkling them with alcohol, either the pure spirit or brandy or vodka. My own solution is to make a plain thick case of some quilted material. This can then be covered by a more decorative outer case.

To go with the pillow at bedtime most of the traditional tisanes will prove relaxing.

AROMATIC AND CLEANSING VINEGARS

So many recipes exist for these, some of them quite complicated, that it is obvious that aromatic vinegars once played an important part in everyday life. The vinegar would act both as a fixative for herb perfumes and as a preservative. Some also believed that it had prophylactic and antiseptic properties. The

vinegars are often described as being 'for the Toilet and the Sick room'. So far as the toilet was concerned, the vinegars were most likely used by those wishing to wash to counteract or to subdue the inevitable smell of stale water drawn from a rainwater butt or tank in summer or in times of drought when the level was getting low. In the sick room the vinegars were used to wash down paintwork, to sprinkle on the bedclothes, furnishings and hangings, to sweeten the air in unventilated rooms within which someone lay ill, among other uses. Some were not aromatic but anti-pestilential — 'the hands and face are washed with it every day; the room fumigated with it, as are also the cloaths, in order to secure the person from infection.'

Above Herb pillows filled with plants such as rosemary, balm, lemon verbena and chamomile have been popular since Victorian times. Hops are considered the best herb to combat insomnia

Today, when these customs are no longer necessary, aromatic vinegars can still be used to sweeten a bath and refresh the bather. And in the bathroom where a commercially produced deodorant is often used to keep the air fresh, a dash of aromatic vinegar in the lavatory basin from time to time might prove to be much more effective and acceptable — and cheaper too.

AROMATIC VINEGAR

From an old recipe, 'Put a handful of rosemary, of wormwod, lavender and mint into a stone jar and cover with a gallon of strong vinegar. Keep near a fire for four days and then strain, add one ounce of powdered camphor. Bottle for use.'

Try the airing cupboard as a substitute for 'keep near a fire.'

ROSE VINEGAR

Half fill a glass jar with scented rose petals. Pour white wine vinegar over these until the jar is full. Cover the mixture and allow it to stand in the hot sun for several days. The minimum is 24 hours of full sunshine. Strain off the liquid and bottle.

Vinegars were also used as a skin astringent and cleanser. Cider vinegar is considered the best kind for this purpose. According to one authority this is because it contains malic acid from the apples from which it is made. These vinegars should be diluted before use, a tablespoonful to 1 litre (2 pints) of water is a rough guide.

LAVENDER VINEGAR

This is simply made. Gather a quantity of lavender flower spikes and put them in a jar. Cover with cider vinegar. Allow to steep for two weeks or more. Strain and bottle.

This is a basic recipe; other herbs can be used in the same way.

HERBS FOR HEALTHY, LUSTROUS HAIR

Many of the herbs which are near to hand can help keep hair and scalp clean, healthy and consequently good looking. Rosemary is generally considered to be the best of all for this purpose, for it is not only a hair tonic and conditioner, but it seems visibly to strengthen the hair, giving it body and lustre and, like sage, another good hair herb, it also darkens the hair. The herbs can easily be made into rinses, of which the following is a good example and guide. Dried herbs can be used but fresh are best.

ROSEMARY HERB RINSE

Strip the leaves from the stems. Place a good handful — a heaped tablespoonful — in a jug and pour on 300ml (½ pint) of boiling water. Allow to steep for a quarter hour. Strain. Use the strained liquid as a final rinse after washing the hair.

Other Herb Rinses

Alternatively, make a herb vinegar in the manner described above (both vinegar and lemon juice are beneficial to hair) using cider vinegar. As a final rinse after washing the hair, use 150ml (¼ pint) to 2 litres (4 pints) of warm water.

Blondes should find that rinses made from chamomile or marigold help keep the hair a good colour and heighten the tints.

Herbs considered especially good for curing dandruff are burdock, southernwood and nettles.

Described as being a tonic for thinning hair are catmint, parsley seed, rosemary and southernwood.

COSMETICS

PARSLEY HONEY FOR AN OILY SKIN

Take 100g (4oz) fresh parsley and 2tsp of thick honey. Wash and remove the stalks from the parsley. Chop finely. A food processor is a great help for this operation. In a mortar pound the parsley further until it is moist. Amalgamate it with the honey. Keep it in a jar in the refrigerator. When required spread it evenly over the skin. Let the pack stay in place for 20–30 minutes, then sponge it off with warm water.

ELDERFLOWER FACE CREAM

Gather a good quantity of elderflowers. Have some ready stripped from their stalks. It is not possible to give precise amounts as the following will make clear. Melt 450g (1lb) pure lard in a heavy saucepan and keep adding the stripped flowers to it until the lard only just covers them. Simmer the two together for an hour or so. Strain through a fine sieve or muslin. Add a few drops of your favourite perfume or oil of lavender. Pour the strained lard into small screw-top jars. Keep in a cool place.

Soothing Herbs and Salves

THYME FOOTBATH
For the foot-weary a thyme footbath should prove to be both refreshing and restorative. Pick a good handful of thyme, or alternatively, if only dried thyme is available, use three table-spoonfuls. Have ready a vessel large enough in which to bathe the feet. Into it put the thyme and a tablespoonful of sea salt. Pour the boiling water on these to a depth sufficient to cover the feet. Allow this to cool until comfortably warm. Soak the feet in it as long as it remains warm. More hot water can be added, of course, if a longer soaking is thought to be beneficial.

HERB SALVE
This is good for bruises, sore and chapped skin. Take 225g (½lb) each of roughly chopped wormwood, elder-flowers and groundsel and 450g (1lb) pure lard.

Mix all the ingredients together, put into an ovenproof pot, bring to the boil in an oven and allow to simmer for half an hour or so. Allow to cool slightly, strain into small pots and cover carefully when cool.

Tonic Drink

Use the tips of young nettles. Protect the hands with thick gloves when picking and handling these. Weigh them. Wash well in two or three waters should they be dusty. To every 450g (1lb) of nettles measure 1 litre (2 pints) of water and boil both together for an hour. Strain through a jelly bag or fine sieve. To every ½ litre (1 pint) of juice add 450g (1lb) sugar. Stir well. Bring to the boil and simmer fast for 30 minutes.

When the syrup is cold pour it into bottles or jars and seal. To drink, add hot water or soda water and ice.

Below Cosmetics made at home by incorporating herbs into a base cream, or by extracting the oils in an infusion are a cheap alternative to buying commercial beauty products and can be tailor-made to your requirements

INDEX

Acknowledgements
The publishers would like to thank Squire's Garden Centre, Twickenham and The Chelsea Gardener, Sydney Street, London SW3 for supplying plants and equipment for the cover photograph.

Picture credits

Steve Bicknell: 31, 85
Bodleian Library: 6
Pat Brindley: 23, 25, 61 (b)
Alan Duns: 64, 68, 70
Mary Evans Picture Library: 78
Iris Hardwick Library: 5, 8 (b), 32, 51, 53, 56, 60 (t), 61 (t)
Leslie Johns: frontispiece, 26, 33, 34, 36, 37, 38, 39, 44 (t,b), 45 (t), 49, 50, 52 (t), 54 (b), 55 (b), 62, 66, 69 (t,b), 73, 74 (b), 75, 77, 79, 80, 81, 83, 84
Maison de Marie Claire/Godeaut: 87
Roger Phillips: 65
David Russell: 35, 41 (b), 42 (t,b), 43 (b), 47 (b), 52 (b), 54 (t), 55 (t), 57 (t), 58, 67
Harry Smith Horticultural Photographic Collection: 9, 10, 11 (t,b), 12, 14 (t,b), 18, 19, 20, 21 (b), 22, 30, 41 (t), 43 (t), 45 (b), 46 (t), 47 (t), 48, 57 (b), 59 (t,b), 60 (b), 63

Artwork

Richard Gliddon: 7
Richard Phipps: 21 (t), 24, 27, 28, 29
Charles Stitt: 16/17